I've Got to Have THAT Recipe, Too!

Enjoy! — *1996*

I've Got to Have THAT Recipe, Too!

Dianne Winsby, Pat Pollard & Barbara Doell

Doubleday Canada Limited, Toronto

Illustrations: Valentino Sanna
Design and typesetting: First Image
Photography: Curtis Lantinga
Printed and bound in Canada

Canadian Cataloguing in Publication Data

Main entry under title:

I've got to have that recipe, too!

ISBN 0-385-25225-0

1. Cookery. I. Doell, Barbara. II. Pollard, Pat.
III. Winsby, Dianne.

TX715.193 1989   641.5   C89-094063-0

Published in Canada by
    Doubleday Canada Limited
    105 Bond Street
    Toronto, Ontario
    M5B 1Y3

Contents

Acknowledgements

The authors would once again like to warmly thank all their near and distant relatives and friends for finding, remembering and sharing this bounty of good tastes.

They would also like to express their appreciation for enduring the repeated phone calls commencing with, "Are you positive that it's a quarter cup of milk, this won't set?"

They would also like to thank Victoria's Fan Tan Gallery, 541 Fisgard Street for their generous loan of folk art, Sasquatch Indian Sweater Shop, 1233 Government Street for the Coast Indian Baskets, Mr. and Mrs. R. Williams of Deep Cove for their rustic kitchen implements, and Doreen Appleton for her heirloom culinary utensils.

They would also particularly like to thank Maggie Reeves of Doubleday Canada for her professional production values and Curtis Lantinga of Toronto, for his inspired photographs.

Be sure to keep a place open on your kitchen shelf for book three!

Introduction

Don't you think that stopping collecting is about twice as hard as starting? It's like your first house. You make a great buy on a seventy-year-old, five-thousand-square-foot monster that "needs work and a little attention." You find out it was formerly used as the headquarters for the road crew of a rock band. Six months of washing and painting and you're ready for the furniture. You try the concrete block and pine board bookcase and the wicker settee, but it isn't quite on the money; off to the auction circuit. Wouldn't oak be nice? And besides, the large pieces are rarely bid on. One sideboard leads to another and in twenty-four months you accumulate enough period furniture to fill the south wing of the Victoria and Albert Museum.

It seems this same tendency to over-collect occurs in the gathering of recipes. One box of aging and tattered five-by-three recipe cards leads to a conversation with an old dear who knows the ingredients for a raspberry and walnut square that had them trying to sneak the recipe just after the great crash of '29 (anything to lift the spirits). The problem is, she can't recall if it was half a cup of vinegar or if she just used the brass dish for measuring, the one that Fred brought back from China . . . you know, the one on the shelf next to the breadbox that measured anything from two tablespoons to two cups, depending on which enamel dragon you fill it to.

So we've done it once more. Another two years searching down rumours of great sauces and breads, trying to get Marge to remember the name and phone number of that short woman that used to come at Christmas, before they moved; you know, the one with the crabapple and currant chutney that Earl used with his spiced beef.

Here it is: the follow-up to *I've GOT to Have That Recipe!*, composed of recipes gathered with care and affection from the diligent search for those who can really cook, who have specialties that are simple and foolproof and that whole families and neighbourhoods have raved about for half a century.

So use this book, have fun and enjoy yourself, secure in the fact that there will be no wasted purchases, no wasted time, no problems and surprisingly little effort. The composing and collecting have been as much fun as our first book.

And by the way, if anyone knows a Mrs. Trapp from Yakima who is somehow related to Pebe's Great-Aunt Glady, could they ask her if the quantity of spinach in her Christmas casserole is half a cup or two cups. It seems the postman left the letter in the rain and that section is pretty smudged!

Great Beginnings

386-Deli
Salad Rolls

The 386-DELI, not a deli but a charming bistro in Victoria, B.C., serves these exotic Vietnamese salad rolls — a spicy combination of seafood, noodles and crisp julienned vegetables, coated in tangy peanut sauce and wrapped up in rice paper. They are fun to make; don't get discouraged if the first few don't work out.

Peanut Sauce:

> 2 - 3 heaping tbsp. fresh ginger, grated
> 8 - 10 cloves garlic, minced
> 2 tbsp. sesame oil*
> 2 tbsp. black bean sauce*
> 1 cup chicken broth
> 1 - 2 tsp. chili paste**
> 1 cup crunchy peanut butter

In a saucepan, over low heat, sauté ginger and garlic in sesame oil for 5 minutes. Add bean sauce and chicken broth and simmer for 15 - 20 minutes. Add chili paste and peanut butter, stir until well blended and smooth. Pour into a glass jar and store in refrigerator until ready to use.

* Sesame oil, black bean sauce and chili paste can be purchased in a Chinese grocery store.
** Chili paste is extremely hot, so please be careful and use sparingly.

Salad Rolls:

The vegetables used here are only a guide. Use your imagination — the combinations are endless.

> 1 1-lb. (500-g) pkg. rice vermicelli*
> (you will only need to use 2 uncooked
> bundles or 3 cups cooked noodles for
> this recipe)
>
> 1 16-oz. (454-g) pkg. rice paper**
> (12 inches in diameter, approximately
> 20 per pkg.)
> 1 recipe Peanut Sauce
> ½ lb. cooked seafood (crab or shrimp)
> 1 - 2 carrots, peeled and julienned
> 1 sweet red pepper, julienned
> 1 green pepper, julienned
> 3 cups iceberg lettuce, finely shredded

Into a large pot of boiling water, drop 2 bundles of rice vermicelli. Cook for 3 - 5 minutes or until done. Drain, rinse under cold water and drain again. Set aside.

To Assemble: Make one complete roll at a time.

In a large bowl of water, dampen 2 rice papers, one at a time, until slightly limp but not soggy. Place on top of each other on counter.

Place 1 heaping tbsp. Peanut Sauce not quite in centre of dampened rice paper, and spread across (about 2 inches wide).

Arrange ⅓ cup of cooked noodles on top of Peanut Sauce.

Arrange pieces of seafood (¼ cup more or less) on top of noodles.

Arrange 2 - 3 strips of each carrot, red pepper and green pepper on top of seafood.

Arrange ¼ cup lettuce on top of vegetables.

Fold end over filling, and then fold in side edges and continue to roll up. Place salad roll, seam-side down, on a cutting board.

Repeat until all ingredients have been used.

To Serve: Cut each salad roll diagonally into 3 serving pieces, and serve with extra Peanut Sauce if you wish.

* Rice vermicelli and rice paper can be purchased in a Chinese grocery store.

** When you become proficient at rolling, only one rice paper is necessary.

Serves 8 - 10.

Cheese-and-Crab-Stuffed French Bread

This is not a dainty hors d'oeuvre!

> 1 loaf French bread
> 2 cups sharp cheddar cheese, grated
> 4 tbsp. butter, softened
> ½ cup mayonnaise
> ¾ - 1 lb. imitation crab or fresh crab,
>   depending on your pocketbook
> Parsley, chopped

Cut bread in half lengthwise. Scoop out some of the bread in each half, leaving a 1-inch shell.

Blend cheese with butter and spread on bread shells.

Add mayonnaise to crab and spread over cheese mixture. Sprinkle with parsley. Place shells on a baking sheet.

Bake at 350°F for 20 minutes or until bubbly. Cut into serving slices.

Makes approximately 16 - 20 pieces.

Heather's
Curried Crab and Cheese
Bread Cups

18 slices white bread, crusts removed
Butter, melted
1 6-oz. can crab
1 cup Holland Edam or Gouda cheese,
   cubed
½ cup carrot, shredded
½ cup mayonnaise
1 tbsp. lemon juice
1 tsp. curry powder
1 tsp. sugar

    Flatten crustless bread with a rolling pin. Mould each slice into cup of muffin tin. Brush with melted butter and bake at 375°F for about 10 minutes or until slightly browned. Cool.
    Mix together remaining ingredients and spoon into bread cups.
    Bake at 375°F for 5 minutes or until heated through. Serve warm or cold.

Makes 18 bread cups.

Norma's
Salmon Mousse

2 7½-oz. cans salmon, skin and bones
    removed
2 envelopes unflavoured gelatine

2 cups mayonnaise
1 tbsp. lemon juice
½ cup chili sauce
¼ cup sweet mixed pickles, chopped
1 tbsp. Worcestershire sauce
1 tsp. dillweed
1 6½-oz. can tuna, drained
4 eggs, hard-cooked and chopped
Salt and pepper to taste
2 - 3 tbsp. fresh parsley, snipped
¼ - ½ cup onion, chopped

Drain salmon and reserve the liquid. In a small saucepan, dissolve gelatine in ½ cup of reserved salmon liquid and cook over low heat until thickened. Set aside.

In a bowl, combine remaining ingredients and mix well. Fold in gelatine mixture and pour into a 6- to 8-cup mold. Chill until set.

Serves 8 or more as a salad and as an appetizer it is endless.

Betty's
Shrimp Coquilles

An oldie but a goodie!

4 tbsp. butter
4 tbsp. flour
2 cups light cream
½ tsp. salt
Freshly ground pepper to taste
½ - ¾ tsp. Worcestershire sauce
Dash cayenne pepper
Dash paprika
2 tbsp. fresh parsley, snipped
2 cups shrimp or other seafood

¼ cup butter, melted
½ cup fine bread crumbs
1 - 2 tbsp. fresh parsley, snipped

In a medium saucepan, melt 4 tbsp. butter, add flour and stir until smooth. Gradually add cream and stir constantly over medium heat until smooth and thickened. Add next 7 ingredients and adjust seasonings to taste. Pour into greased individual shells or ramekins.

Combine ¼ cup melted butter, bread crumbs and parsley. Sprinkle on top of each shrimp dish and bake at 350°F for 20 minutes or until bubbly.

Serves 8.

Barbara's
Pickled Salmon

10 lb. salmon
4-5 lb. rock salt

2-3 lb. small onions, peeled and sliced into
rings

Pickling Solution:

6 cups white vinegar
$3\frac{3}{4}$ cups sugar
48 whole allspice, crushed

Fillet salmon and cut into lengths to fit in a crock or plastic container. (Do not use a metal container.)

Place a generous layer of rock salt in bottom of crock, top with salmon pieces, layer with lots of rock salt, top with salmon. Repeat until all salmon has been layered, ending with rock salt. Overdo the rock salt rather than underdo. Place a plate plus a weight (rock or brick) on top.

After 24 hours, add enough water to cover all layers. Let sit in brine at least two weeks.

After 2 weeks, remove salmon from brine. Remove skin and any lateral bones. *Thinly* slice salmon across grain at a slanted angle*, starting at the top of the head end. Cut each thin strip into 2-inch lengths. Rinse in cold water (at least 4 times) to desired saltiness.

In covered containers, place a generous layer of onion rings, top with salmon slices and repeat until jar is filled.

Combine ingredients for pickling solution until well blended. Pour solution over onion-salmon layers and cover and refrigerate.

Let jars marinate at least 4 days before consuming.

Keeps indefinitely in refrigerator.

*Cutting salmon across grain at a slanted angle is important as it keeps pieces in strips.

Makes 2-3 quarts.

Chicken Cheese Ball

If you have any leftover (which we doubt you will), this is tasty as a sandwich filling.

1 8-oz. (250-g) pkg. cream cheese,
   softened
2 cups cheddar cheese, grated
1 cup Monterey Jack cheese, grated
$\frac{1}{4}$ cup dairy sour cream
$\frac{1}{2}$ cup green onions, chopped finely
1 6$\frac{1}{2}$-oz. can flaked chicken, drained and
   flaked
1 tsp. Worcestershire sauce
4 - 5 drops Tabasco

Fresh parsley, snipped
Pecans, chopped

Blend all ingredients together except parsley and pecans. Form into a ball.

Roll in snipped parsley and chopped pecans. Cover and chill until ready to serve.

Serve with crackers or melba toast rounds.

Serves 8 - 10.

 # Chili-Cheese Dip

2 tbsp. butter
1 large onion, chopped
1 clove garlic, minced
1 14-oz. can tomatoes, drained and
    chopped
1 4-oz. can diced green chilies

2 tbsp. butter
2 tbsp. flour
1 cup cream

12 - 14 slices bacon, cooked and crumbled
1½ lb. cheddar cheese, grated
    (or ½ Monterey Jack and ½ cheddar)
Tabasco
Salt and pepper

In a medium-sized skillet, melt 2 tbsp. butter and sauté onion and garlic until onion is transparent. Add tomatoes and chilies and simmer for 5 minutes.

In a small saucepan, melt 2 tbsp. butter, add flour and stir until smooth. Gradually add cream and stir constantly over medium heat until smooth and thickened.

Pour white sauce into onion-tomato mixture. Add bacon, cheese and seasonings to taste. Stir until bubbly and cheese is melted.

Serve hot (in a chafing dish) with Homemade Tortilla Chips (page 23) or buy your favourite brand.

Serves 15 - 20.

Herbed Hot Camembert

Company is coming in ten minutes? Simply whip up this terrific appetizer.

>1 can Camembert cheese
>Melted butter
>*Fines herbes**

Open can and unwrap cheese; set cheese aside. Generously coat inside of can with melted butter and sprinkle with *fines herbes*.

Return cheese to can and coat top of cheese with melted butter and more *fines herbes*.

Place can of cheese on a baking sheet and bake at 350°F for 10 minutes. Remove from oven, immediately invert can onto a serving plate and let stand for 10 minutes. Remove can — cheese should be slightly puffed up.

Serve immediately with melba toast rounds or crackers.

* *Fines herbes* are available in the spice section of most grocery stores.

Serves 4.

Marnee's Almonds

Don't stop after making one batch — keep on batching. Your friends will love you!

>2 cups whole blanched almonds*
>1 cup white sugar
>4 tbsp. butter
>1 tsp. vanilla extract
>$1\frac{1}{2}$ tsp. salt

Heat almonds, sugar and butter in a heavy skillet over medium heat. Stir and cook until almonds are toasted and sugar has turned golden brown (about 15 minutes). Remove from heat and immediately stir in vanilla. Quickly spread nuts onto aluminum foil or greased baking sheet and sprinkle with salt. Cool and break into pieces.

* Some people prefer unblanched almonds.

Makes 2 cups.

Mexican
Artichoke Chili Puff Baked in a Bread Shell

1 round loaf of bread, such as
    pumpernickel

1 14-oz. can artichoke hearts, packed in
    water, drained and chopped
1 4-oz. can diced green chilies, drained
1 cup mayonnaise
½ cup Parmesan cheese, grated
¾ cup sharp cheddar cheese, grated

¼ cup sharp cheddar cheese, grated

Cut a lid from top of round loaf of bread and reserve. Scoop out centre of bread to make a bowl shape and reserve.

In a medium bowl, blend all filling ingredients together. Spoon filling into bread shell and sprinkle with ¼ cup grated cheese. Place on a baking sheet and bake at 350°F for 15 - 20 minutes.

Cut reserved bread into serving pieces to serve with chili puff.

Serves 6 - 10.

Samosas

These spicy little East Indian appetizers are fun to make with a friend as they are fiddly. But what results! Although best served immediately, they can be prepared early in the day and reheated in a warm oven.

1½ lb. lean ground beef
1 medium onion, finely chopped
1 green pepper, finely chopped
1½ tsp. fresh ginger, grated
1 clove garlic, minced
1 tsp. mint sauce
⅓ tsp. cayenne pepper
1 tsp. coriander
½ tsp. cumin
⅓ tsp. dried ginger
Salt and pepper to taste
½ cup currants
½ cup almonds, chopped

1 - 2 pkg. (16-oz.) won ton covers, thawed
  if frozen
Oil for deep frying

In a heavy skillet, brown meat. Drain off any excess fat. Add onion and green pepper and cook until onion is transparent. Add remaining ingredients and cook over low heat for 20 minutes.

Place up to 2 tsp. of filling in centre of each won ton cover. Moisten edges with water and fold won ton cover in half to make a triangular shape. Seal edges with a fork. Repeat until all of filling has been used. As you work, keep the won ton pastry covered with a damp cloth to prevent it from drying out. (Samosas can be frozen at this stage for up to one month.)

Drop samosas, a few at a time, into hot (350°F) oil (about 2 inches deep) and cook until brown. Watch carefully. Remove with a slotted spoon and drain on paper towel.

Serve hot with Crabapple Chili Sauce or chutney of your choice.

Serves a crowd.

Crabapple Chili Sauce

1 12-oz. jar crabapple jelly
2 tbsp. vinegar
1 heaping tbsp. brown sugar
1 tbsp. green onion, finely chopped
1 tsp. dried crushed red pepper flakes
1 clove garlic, minced (optional)
$\frac{1}{2}$ - 1 tsp. fresh ginger root, grated

In a saucepan, combine all ingredients and bring to a boil, stirring constantly. Remove from heat and serve hot with Samosas.
To store, keep refrigerated in a covered jar.

Onion Puffs

Delicious and inexpensive!

8 slices white bread
5 very small white onions
$\frac{1}{2}$ cup or more mayonnaise
Parmesan cheese, grated
6 - 10 slices bacon, chopped into small
pieces and slightly undercooked

Cut four circles out of each slice of bread (the size of a spice jar lid). Place bread circles on a greased baking sheet. Thinly slice onions and arrange a slice on top of each circle. Spread generously with mayonnaise and sprinkle with Parmesan cheese. Top with cooked bacon bits.
Bake at 375°F for 15 - 20 minutes.

Makes 32 appetizers.

Puff Pastry
Spinach Tarts

These can be served as an appetizer or as a luncheon dish accompanied with a green salad or fresh fruit slices. This recipe can be easily doubled or tripled.

1 10-oz. pkg. frozen patty shells

2 eggs, well beaten
1 10-oz. pkg. frozen chopped spinach,
  thawed and well drained (the water
  should be squeezed out)
$\frac{1}{4}$ cup light cream
$\frac{1}{4}$ tsp. garlic salt
$\frac{1}{4}$ tsp. dillweed
2 tbsp. onion, minced
1$\frac{3}{4}$ cups Swiss cheese, grated

Prepare pastry shells as instructed on package. Undercook slightly. Remove lids from pastry shells and set aside.

In a bowl, beat eggs and add spinach, cream, garlic salt, dillweed, onion and 1$\frac{1}{4}$ cups grated Swiss cheese. Spoon spinach mixture into pastry shells, pressing the mixture in gently. (Replace lid on top of each if you wish.)

Bake at 350°F for approximately 15 minutes or until golden brown. Remove from oven, sprinkle on remaining cheese and bake for 5 minutes longer or until cheese is melted.

Makes 6 individual pastry shells.

Homemade Tortilla Chips

2 cups oil
2 10-oz. pkg. corn or flour tortillas (10 per
    pkg.)
Salt

Sausage Dip Olé

In a heavy Dutch oven or electric frying pan, heat oil to 375°F
(a 1-inch cube of bread dropped in oil should become golden brown
in 60 seconds).

Cut each tortilla into 8 triangles. Drop triangles, 8 - 10 at a time, into
preheated oil and cook, turning occasionally, until golden brown.
Watch carefully — they cook very quickly. Drain on paper towel, shake
on salt and serve warm or cold with Sausage Dip Olé.

The chips will keep in a sealed plastic bag, but are best fresh.

Approximately 160 chips.

Sausage Dip Olé

*Served with lots of ice-cold Canadian beer, this hearty Mexican
appetizer is great for the Grey Cup Party, especially when the game
goes into overtime!*

1 lb. lean ground beef
1 lb. lean ground pork
1 medium onion, minced
2 lb. Velveeta cheese
1 8-oz. jar medium salsa sauce*
2 tbsp. diced green chilies
1 10-oz. can condensed cream of
    mushroom soup
1 tsp. garlic powder

In a Dutch oven, combine beef, pork and onion, and cook until meat
is browned and onion is transparent. Drain well.

Melt cheese in top of a double boiler or in a microwave oven, and
add to meat mixture. Add rest of ingredients and mix well.

Serve warm in a chafing dish with Homemade Tortilla Chips.
(Substitute "store bought" if you are rushed for time.)

* If you like it hot, substitute hot salsa sauce.

Serves a crowd.

Sandy's
Escargot Pâté

This wonderful pâté freezes well.

1 8-oz. (250-g) can escargot

½ cup cold butter, divided
2 - 3 tbsp. dry white wine or vermouth
3 cloves garlic, minced

4 oz. cream cheese, cold
2 green onions, chopped
¼ cup fresh parsley, snipped
Pepper to taste

Rinse escargot and set aside to drain.

Heat ¼ cup butter in a small saucepan. Add wine, garlic and escargot and bring to a boil. Immediately reduce heat, cover and simmer for 5 minutes.

Cube ¼ cup butter and cream cheese and put into a blender or food processor. Add onion, parsley and pepper. Add hot mixture and process until finely chopped and well blended.

Spoon into a serving dish, cover and refrigerate for at least 2 hours. If you think the pâté is too thick, add a little more wine. Serve with crackers.

Makes 1½ cups.

Soups

Cream of Broccoli Soup with Port and Almonds

A delicious and elegant luncheon soup.

2 tbsp. butter
1½ cups leeks or onions, chopped
2 cups broccoli, trimmed and chopped,
　　including peeled stems
1 cup potatoes, peeled and chopped
4 cups chicken broth
¼ cup ground almonds, toasted (optional)
1 cup light cream
Salt and freshly ground pepper to taste
1½ - 2 oz. port wine

Melt butter in a large saucepan, add vegetables and sauté over medium heat for 5 minutes. Add broth and simmer for 20 minutes or until done.

Purée vegetable mixture in a blender, return to saucepan and add almonds and light cream. Simmer over medium heat until just heated through. Add salt and pepper to taste and port. Stir well and serve.

Serves 4.

Joan's Hunters' Soup

This soup ages beautifully. We think it tastes better three days after it has been made. It's a meal in itself — just add crusty buns. Freezes well, too.

2 - 3 lb. stewing beef
8 cups water
1 28-oz. can tomatoes or 6 large tomatoes
　　with skins removed
4 carrots, peeled and cut into chunks
5 potatoes, peeled and cut into chunks
4 large stalks celery with leaves, chopped
1 large onion, chopped
¼ - ½ small cabbage, sliced thickly
⅓ cup pot barley
Salt and freshly ground pepper to taste

Cut stewing beef into bite-size chunks and place in a Dutch oven or large pot. Cover with water. Bring to a boil, then reduce heat, cover and simmer meat until tender, approximately 1 - 1½ hours. When the meat is tender, add remaining ingredients. Bring to a boil, cover and simmer for 30 minutes or until vegetables are done. Adjust seasonings and serve.

Serves 6 - 8.

Baked French Leek Soup

A nice change from French onion soup.

> 4 tbsp. butter
> 5 medium leeks, washed and sliced,
>   ½-inch thick
> 2 - 3 tbsp. flour
> 4 cups chicken broth
>   (3 10-oz. cans)
> Salt and freshly ground pepper to taste
>
> 4 slices crusty white bread
> ⅔ cup Swiss cheese, grated

Melt butter in a large saucepan. Add leeks, sauté and stir until transparent and tender. Sprinkle flour over mixture and mix in well.

In a small saucepan, heat broth until hot and pour over leek mixture, stirring until smooth. Add salt and pepper and simmer, covered, for 15 - 20 minutes.

Lightly toast bread and place in individual soup bowls. Sprinkle a little of the cheese over each slice, add the soup and sprinkle on remaining cheese.

Place the bowls on a baking sheet and bake at 325°F for 10 - 15 minutes. Serve immediately.

Serves 4.

 # Carrot Soup

2 medium onions, chopped
$\frac{1}{4}$ cup butter
6 medium carrots, peeled and cut into
  chunks
1 medium potato, peeled and cut into
  chunks
2 10-oz. cans chicken broth
2 10-oz. cans water
Salt and freshly ground pepper to taste
$\frac{1}{4}$ tsp. nutmeg
$\frac{1}{2}$ cup dry white wine (optional)

$\frac{3}{4}$ cup heavy cream
Fresh mint or parsley for garnish

In a large saucepan, sauté onions in butter until tender. Add carrots, potatoes, broth and water. Cover and simmer until vegetables are fork tender (20 - 30 minutes). Pour into a blender and purée. Add salt, pepper, nutmeg and wine.

To serve, reheat almost to a boil. Spoon into individual soup bowls. Pour 2 tbsp. cream into centre of each bowl and garnish with fresh mint or parsley.

Serves 6.

Linda's Cucumber Soup

2 8-inch English cucumbers
2 tbsp. butter
$\frac{1}{4}$ cup green onions, chopped
4 cups chicken broth (3 10-oz. cans)
1 tbsp. white wine vinegar
$\frac{1}{2}$ - $\frac{3}{4}$ tsp. dried tarragon
3 tbsp. Cream of Wheat (quick-cooking)
Salt and freshly ground pepper to taste
1 cup dairy sour cream

Cut 12 slices of cucumber with skin on for garnish and set aside. Peel remaining cucumbers and chop into chunks.

Melt butter in a medium saucepan, add green onions and sauté for 1 minute. Add cucumber chunks, broth, vinegar and tarragon and

gradually bring to a boil. Stir in Cream of Wheat and simmer, uncovered, for 20 minutes. Pour into blender and purée. If too thick, add a small amount of broth or milk. Season to taste, gently blend in sour cream and reheat. (Do not boil.) Garnish with slices of cucumber and serve immediately.

Serves 4 - 6.

Fresh Tomato Gumbo with Crab and Gin

A hearty soup, full of flavour!

8 tbsp. butter
3 lb. ripe tomatoes, quartered
4 stalks celery with leaves, chopped
1 large onion, chopped
3 large carrots, peeled and cut into chunks
2 leeks, chopped
3 cloves garlic, minced
1 tbsp. tarragon
6 tbsp. fresh parsley, snipped
½ tsp. basil
½ tsp. thyme
2 bay leaves
⅓ cup white wine

2 10-oz. cans chicken broth
2 cups water
1 cup uncooked white rice
Salt and freshly ground pepper to taste

1 7-oz. can crab or other seafood
¼ cup gin

In a large Dutch oven, melt butter, add next 12 ingredients and sauté for 20 minutes. Add broth, water and rice, cover and cook over medium heat until rice is cooked (about 30 minutes). Reduce heat and simmer for 1 - 2 hours. Add crab or other seafood and gin. Adjust seasonings, remove bay leaves and serve.

Serves 6 - 8.

 # Pumpkin Soup

2 tbsp. butter
$\frac{1}{4}$ cup onion, finely chopped
$1\frac{3}{4}$ cups cooked pumpkin (canned or
   fresh)
2 10-oz. cans chicken broth
$2\frac{1}{2}$ cups light cream
$\frac{1}{8}$ tsp. ground cloves
$\frac{1}{2}$ tsp. sugar
1 tsp. lemon juice
3 - 4 drops Tabasco
Salt and freshly ground pepper to taste

Butter
Freshly ground nutmeg

Melt butter in a large saucepan, add onions and sauté until transparent. Add next 9 ingredients, stir until blended. Bring almost to a boil, then simmer for 10 - 15 minutes. (Do not boil.)

Serve hot with a dollop of butter and a dash of freshly ground nutmeg.

Serves 4 - 6.

Salads
and Dressings

Stockbroker's Spinach Salad

Sandy, our stockbroker, says this salad is preferred by Bulls, Bears and Inside Traders!

Salad:

> 1 bunch fresh spinach, washed, dried and
> torn into bite-size pieces
> 1 green apple, cored and chopped
> 1 cup salted peanuts

Dressing:

> ¼ cup lemon juice
> 2 tbsp. red wine vinegar
> 4 tbsp. mango chutney
> ¾ tsp. curry powder
> ⅛ tsp. cayenne pepper
> ½ tsp. sugar
> ½ tsp. salt
> ¾ cup olive oil

Salad: Combine salad ingredients in a bowl and toss.

Dressing: In a blender, combine all ingredients except oil and blend well (about 2 minutes). Gradually add oil and blend until smooth. Pour enough dressing over salad to taste, toss and serve.

Serves 4.

386-Deli Salad Rolls (*see recipe page 10-11*)

 # Super Salad

What can we tell you . . . this is a SUPER salad!

Salad:

> 4 cups romaine lettuce, washed and dried
> 2 cups spinach, washed and dried
> 2 cups fresh mushrooms, sliced
> 1 medium sweet red pepper, sliced in thin strips
> ½ cup pumpkin seeds,* toasted
> ½ cup feta cheese, crumbled
> 6 slices bacon, cooked and crumbled (optional)

Dressing:

> 2 cloves garlic, peeled
> 2 tsp. liquid honey
> 6 tbsp. cider vinegar
> 9 tbsp. salad oil
> Salt and freshly ground pepper to taste
> ¼ - ½ tsp. paprika

Salad: Tear romaine and spinach into bite-size pieces, add remaining ingredients and toss with dressing.

Dressing: Put dressing ingredients in a blender and process until thick and frothy.

* Pumpkin seeds can be purchased in health food stores.

Serves 8 - 10.

Carrot Soup (*see page* 28)

Kevin's
Flaming Spinach Salad

Salad:

> 2 bunches fresh spinach, washed, dried
>   and torn into bite-size pieces
> 1 lb. bacon, cooked and crumbled, reserve
>   fat for dressing
> 3 hard-cooked eggs, grated

Dressing:

> $\frac{2}{3}$ cup bacon fat
> $\frac{1}{3}$ cup white wine vinegar
> 2 tbsp. lemon juice
> 1 tbsp. Worcestershire sauce
> Salt and pepper to taste
> $\frac{1}{4}$ tsp. tarragon, crushed
>
> 2 - 3 oz. brandy

Salad: Toss salad ingredients in a salad bowl.

Dressing: In a small saucepan, combine dressing ingredients and heat to a boil.

In another saucepan, heat brandy briefly and then flame. Add immediately to hot dressing.

Pour flaming dressing over salad and serve immediately.

Serves 8.

Wendy's
Japanese Coleslaw

This very different salad can be made and dressed the day before if you wish — it keeps well in the refrigerator.

Salad:

½ cup sliced almonds, toasted
2 tbsp. sesame seeds, toasted
1 large cabbage, shredded
2½ cups bean sprouts
2 cups fresh mushrooms, sliced
1 bunch green onions, chopped
¼ cup sunflower seeds
1 pkg. Ichiban chicken flavour noodles,
    crumbled (save seasoning for dressing)

Dressing:

Seasoning from noodles
½ cup salad oil
½ cup soya sauce
4 tbsp. vinegar
3 tbsp. sugar
Salt and freshly ground pepper to taste

Salad: Combine salad ingredients and add dressing. Mix well.
Dressing: Combine dressing ingredients in a glass jar and shake well.

Serves 10 - 12.

Barb's
Jellied Coleslaw

Not just another jellied salad — even kids love this one!

1 3-oz. pkg. lime gelatine
½ cup boiling water
1 tbsp. white vinegar

1¼ cups cabbage, grated
1 cup carrot, grated
½ cup celery, finely chopped
3 green onions, finely chopped
¼ cup Miracle Whip

Dissolve gelatine in water, stir in vinegar and let set until syrupy.
Combine vegetables and add to gelatine. Stir in Miracle Whip. Pour into a 4-cup mold.
Refrigerate for several hours until set. Unmold and serve.

Serves 6.

Chicken Salad
à la Grapes and Cashews

Salad:

> 2 cups seedless green grapes
> 4 cups chicken breast, poached and diced

Dressing:

> 1 cup dairy sour cream
> 1 cup mayonnaise
> 4 tbsp. green onions, finely chopped
> 2 tbsp. lemon juice
> 2 tsp. curry powder
> ½ tsp. salt (optional)
>
> 2 - 3 cups cashews
> Shredded lettuce to line salad plates
>   (optional)
> Green grapes for garnish (optional)

Salad: In a large bowl, combine grapes and chicken.

Dressing: In bowl, combine sour cream, mayonnaise, onion, lemon juice, curry and salt. Blend well. Pour dressing over chicken and grapes, mix well and refrigerate until ready to serve.

To serve: Stir cashews into salad. Serve on shredded lettuce on individual plates and garnish with grapes.

Serves 8 as a luncheon salad.

Cobb Salad

Everyone has their favourite Cobb Salad recipe — this is ours.
Remember to finely shred or chop all ingredients.

Salad:

> ½ head iceberg lettuce, shredded
> ½ head romaine lettuce, shredded
> 3 - 4 small tomatoes, finely chopped
> 2 - 3 tbsp. chives or green onion tops, minced
> 2½ cups chicken breast,* poached and diced
> 6 - 10 slices bacon, cooked until crisp and crumbled
> 2 hard-cooked eggs, finely chopped
> 3 oz. blue cheese, crumbled
> 1 - 2 avocados, peeled and finely chopped
>
> Lettuce leaves for lining salad plates (optional)

Dressing:

> 1⅓ cup salad oil
> ⅔ cup vinegar
> 1 clove garlic, minced
> 1 tsp. salt
> ½ tsp. freshly ground pepper
> 1 tsp. sugar
> 1 tsp. dry mustard
> 1 tsp. paprika
> 1 tsp. Worcestershire sauce

Salad: Mix salad ingredients in a large salad bowl. Just before serving add about half of the dressing to salad. Toss lightly to see if you need more dressing. Serve immediately.

Dressing: Combine dressing ingredients in a large jar with a lid. Shake vigorously and refrigerate until ready to use. This dressing could also be made in a food processor.

* Leftover chicken or turkey breast can be substituted.

Serves 6 for luncheon.

 # Oriental Chicken and Grape Salad

Salad:

3 tbsp. butter, melted
1 tsp. garlic salt
2 tsp. Worcestershire sauce
3 cups dry chow mein noodles

3 cups snow peas, cut diagonally in strips
6 green onions, cut diagonally
4 chicken breast halves, poached* and
    diagonally sliced (3 cups)
2 cups seedless green grapes
1 8-oz. can water chestnuts, sliced and
    drained
1 14-oz. can baby corn cobs, cut in half
    and drained
2 tbsp. sesame seeds, toasted
1 cup flaked almonds, toasted

Dressing:

1 clove garlic, minced
1 tsp. Worcestershire sauce
$\frac{1}{3}$ cup fresh parsley, snipped
1 cup mayonnaise
$\frac{1}{2}$ tsp. dry mustard
3 tbsp. white wine vinegar
$\frac{1}{2}$ cup dairy sour cream
1 tbsp. soya sauce

Salad: In a large bowl, mix butter, salt and Worcestershire together. Stir in noodles and toss to coat well. Spread onto a baking sheet and bake at 250°F for 15 minutes. Set aside.

Toss remaining ingredients with noodles in a large salad bowl. Pour dressing over salad and toss again.

Dressing: Combine dressing ingredients in a blender and process until smooth.

* To poach chicken breasts, place skinned chicken into boiling water, broth or white wine to cover. Simmer gently for 15 minutes or until tender.

Serves 6 - 8.

Pasta Salad with Spicy Italian Vinaigrette

This salad is a wonderful concoction of pasta, fresh vegetables, meat and cheese with a spicy Italian vinaigrette. The recipe is only a guide. Make your own creation — the combinations are endless. It is best served at room temperature after marinating for several hours or overnight in the refrigerator. Enjoy with a bottle of wine and a loaf of crusty bread.

Salad:

1 lb. pasta, such as spinach rotini or ½ lb. spinach fettucine and ½ lb. rotini
¼ cup olive oil

2 - 3 cups broccoli, cut into chunks
2 - 3 cups cauliflower, cut into chunks
1 - 2 carrots, peeled and coarsely shredded
5 green onions, chopped
1 cup red onion, coarsely chopped
1 4-inch zucchini, cut into chunks
1 small green pepper, coarsely chopped
1 small red pepper, coarsely chopped
15 - 20 snow peas
10 - 15 cherry tomatoes
1 cup fresh basil, chopped
1 cup fresh parsley, snipped
¼ - ½ lb. pepper salami
½ cup Parmesan cheese, grated (optional)
Salt and pepper to taste (optional)

Dressing:

¼ cup olive oil
¼ cup vegetable oil
¼ cup white wine vinegar or 3 tbsp. white wine vinegar and 1 tbsp. balsamic vinegar*
3 - 4 cloves garlic, minced
1 heaping tbsp. Dijon mustard
1 tsp. Worcestershire sauce, or to taste
Salt and freshly ground pepper to taste

Salad: In a large pot, bring 4 qt. water to a boil, drop in pasta all at once, stir several times to separate pieces and cook until tender but firm. Drain, rinse in cold water and drain again. Put pasta in a large salad bowl, toss with ¼ cup olive oil and bring to room temperature, tossing a few more times to be sure the pasta doesn't stick together.

Blanch broccoli and cauliflower until just tender. Chill. (Some people prefer not to blanch the broccoli or cauliflower.)

Add broccoli, cauliflower and remaining ingredients to pasta and toss with vinaigrette dressing. Marinate for several hours and serve at room temperature.

Dressing: Combine dressing ingredients in a glass jar and shake well. This dressing can be stored in a sealed jar in the refrigerator.

* Balsamic vinegar can be purchased at specialty food shops.

Serves 8 - 12.

Susan's Onion Salad

A deliciously different make-ahead salad. The sugar causes the onion to "weep" and this, with the mayonnaise, makes the dressing.

> 3 - 4 medium onions
> 4 or more tbsp. sugar
>
> 1 head iceberg lettuce, torn into bite-size
>   pieces
> ½ - 1 cup mayonnaise
>
> ½ - ¾ cup Monterey Jack white cheese,
>   cubed
> 6 or more slices bacon, cooked until crisp
>   and crumbled

Slice onions and separate into rings. Lay out onion rings on a tray and sprinkle with sugar. Set aside.

In a medium-sized bowl, place one-third of the lettuce and dab with approximately ⅓ cup mayonnaise. Layer with one-third of the onions. Repeat layers, ending with onions. Cover and refrigerate for 3 or more hours.

Just before serving, toss cheese with salad and sprinkle bacon on top for garnish.

Serves 6.

Lorna's
Sauerkraut Salad

Make this salad the day before your luncheon. It keeps for a long time in the refrigerator.

Salad:

> 1 32-oz. jar sauerkraut, drained
> 2 cups celery, chopped
> 1 large onion, chopped
> 1 large green pepper, chopped
> 1 tbsp. poppy seed
> 1 tbsp. mustard seed
> ½ tsp. celery seed

Dressing:

> 1½ cups sugar
> ½ cup and 1 tbsp. vinegar
> ½ cup salad oil

   Salad: Combine salad ingredients and add dressing. Mix well. Leave salad in refrigerator for 24 hours. Drain to serve.
   Dressing: Put dressing ingredients in a small saucepan, and bring to a boil for 1 minute. Cool and pour over salad.

Serves 6 - 8.

Vegetables

Old-Fashioned
Onions in Cheese Sauce

Grandma's recipe!

20 - 24 small onions

Sauce:

2 tbsp. butter
2 tbsp. flour
1½ cups milk
1½ cups sharp cheddar cheese, grated
½ tsp. dry mustard
Salt and freshly ground pepper to taste

Boil onions in water for 5 - 10 minutes. Drain and place in a greased baking dish.

Sauce: In a saucepan, melt butter over low heat. Blend in flour, stirring until smooth. Gradually whisk in milk. Heat to boiling, stirring constantly until mixture is smooth and thickened. Add remaining ingredients and stir over low heat until cheese is melted and sauce is smooth. Pour over onions and bake at 350°F for 20 - 30 minutes or until onions are fork tender.

Serves 6 - 8.

Red Cabbage, Apples and Onions

This spicy, crunchy combination of interesting ingredients can be served hot as a vegetable dish, but is also good cold.

1 medium head red cabbage, shredded
¼ cup butter
1 large onion, chopped
4 medium green apples
2 cups water
2 tbsp. cider vinegar
3 tbsp. lemon juice
½ tsp. nutmeg
1½ - 2 tsp. salt
1½ - 2 tsp. pepper
½ - ¾ cup raisins (optional)

In a large Dutch oven, sauté shredded cabbage in butter for 15 minutes. Add remaining ingredients and cook for a further 15 minutes, stirring occasionally. The cabbage should remain slightly crunchy. Do not overcook.

Makes 10 - 12 small servings.

Apples and Onions

Perfect with pork!

2 medium onions, sliced and separated
    into rings
½ cup butter
½ cup cold water
4 large apples, cored, peeled and sliced
2 tbsp. brown sugar
½ cup seedless light raisins
Dash of cloves, nutmeg and cinnamon
Salt and pepper to taste

In a large skillet, sauté onions in butter. Add water before onions brown. Add apples, sugar and raisins. Cover and steam for 3 minutes. Sprinkle lightly with spices and seasonings and serve immediately.

Serves 6.

Mrs. Weiss's
Vegetable Medley

So you think this sounds too easy . . . try it! This recipe doubles or triples easily.

> 3 - 4 cups zucchini, cubed
> 1 medium red onion, sliced
> 2 cups fresh mushrooms, sliced
> 2 large tomatoes, coarsely chopped
> 1 - 2 cloves garlic, minced
> 1 - 2 tsp. oregano
> 1 cup sharp cheddar cheese, grated
> 1 cup mozzarella cheese, grated
>
> Extra grated cheese for topping

Combine all ingredients and place in a greased baking dish. Top with extra cheese. Bake, uncovered, at 350°F for 30 minutes. Do not overcook.

Serves 4 - 6.

Isabel's
Turnip Casserole

A favourite for Christmas dinner because it is made a day ahead.

2 - 3 medium turnips or rutabagas (we
  use yellow rutabagas)
1 cup applesauce
6 tbsp. butter
4 tsp. brown sugar
1 tsp. salt
¼ tsp. pepper
2 eggs, beaten
1¾ cups soft bread crumbs
        combined with
2 tbsp. butter, melted

Peel, chunk and cook turnip until fork tender. Drain and mash well.
Beat to a smooth consistency. Add remaining ingredients except bread-
crumb mixture. Divide bread-crumb mixture in half and add one-half
to turnip mixture. Combine well. Spoon into a greased 2-qt. casserole.
Sprinkle with remaining bread crumbs, cover and refrigerate overnight.
  Bake uncovered at 350°F for 1 hour.

Serves 10 - 12.

Easy Parmesan Potato Wedges

Teenagers' favourite — aren't we all teenagers at heart? This recipe can be doubled or tripled and can be served with sour cream if you wish.

⅓ cup parmesan cheese, grated
1 tsp. paprika
1 tsp. garlic powder
½ tsp. salt
¼ - ½ tsp. pepper

4 potatoes, unpeeled
⅓ cup vegetable oil

In a plastic bag, combine first 5 ingredients.

Cut each unpeeled potato into 8 wedges. Dip wedges in oil and then shake in cheese mixture. Place wedges on a baking sheet skin side down.

Bake at 400°F for 30 - 40 minutes.

4 servings.

Baked Potato Balls

2 cups mashed potatoes,* chilled
1 egg, beaten
Cornflakes, crushed
Butter

Combine potatoes and egg and mix well. Shape into 4 balls and roll in crushed cornflakes. Make a depression on top of each ball and dot with butter.

Place on a greased baking sheet and bake at 425°F for 20 minutes or until brown.

Variation: Try adding chives or grated cheese to the mashed potatoes.

* When mashing potatoes, add a little butter, salt and pepper to taste.

Serves 4.

Carrots in Ginger Cream

What to do with plain old carrots?

5 medium carrots

2 - 3 tbsp. butter
1 tsp. fresh ginger root, grated
Salt and pepper to taste
¼ cup reserved carrot liquid

¼ cup light cream
1 egg yolk
1 tsp. sugar

1 tbsp. fresh parsley, snipped

Cut carrots into matchstick pieces. Cook in boiling water for 3 minutes. Drain, reserving ¼ cup liquid.

In a large skillet, melt butter, add grated ginger and cook for 1 minute. Add carrots, salt and pepper, and toss to coat. Pour in reserved liquid, cover and simmer for 2 - 3 minutes.

In a small bowl, beat cream, egg yolk and sugar. Stir into carrots. Heat through, uncovered, but do not boil.

Remove from heat, sprinkle with parsley and serve.

Variation: Add 1 5-oz. can water chestnuts, sliced and drained before serving.

Serves 4.

Mushroom Harvest

Great with steak.

1 lb. fresh mushrooms, sliced
½ small cauliflower, sliced
1 8-10-inch zucchini, unpeeled and sliced
   ¼ inch thick
2 large stalks of celery, sliced ¼-inch
   diagonally
1 medium green pepper, cut in ¼-inch
   strips
2 large carrots, peeled and sliced
   diagonally
1 bunch green onions, chopped

4 tbsp. butter
1 chicken or beef bouillon cube, crumbled
3 tbsp. water
Pepper to taste

Prepare vegetables and store in a plastic bag in refrigerator until cooking time.

Melt butter in a large skillet with a lid. Over high heat, sauté vegetables for 3 - 5 minutes, stirring continuously. Reduce heat and add bouillon, water and pepper. Cover tightly and simmer for 2 minutes until tender but still crisp. Do not overcook. Serve hot.

Serves 8.

Chinese-Style
Sesame Broccoli

3 tbsp. vegetable oil
1 small onion, finely chopped
1 lb. broccoli, including stems, cut into
   1-inch chunks
2 tbsp. soya sauce
1 tsp. sugar

1 tsp. cornstarch
½ cup chicken broth

Salt and pepper to taste
1 - 2 tbsp. sesame seeds, toasted

In a large skillet or wok, heat oil, add onion and sauté until tender. Add broccoli and cook, stirring constantly, for 3 minutes. Add soya sauce and sugar.

In a measuring cup, blend cornstarch and chicken broth and add to broccoli, stirring over medium to high heat for 1 more minute. Add salt and pepper to taste. Sprinkle with toasted sesame seeds and serve immediately.

Variation: Add a handful of snow peas or a small can of sliced water chestnuts.

Serves 4.

Tomato Scallop

We always serve this with barbecued or baked salmon. The recipe can be doubled or tripled.

2½ cups soda crackers, crushed
1 28-oz. can tomatoes, undrained
2 cups sharp cheddar cheese, grated
¼ cup Parmesan cheese, grated
¼ tsp. pepper
1 tsp. salt
1 tsp. oregano
½ tsp. garlic powder
1 tsp. Worcestershire sauce
1 tsp. H.P. sauce
1 tbsp. fresh parsley, snipped

Topping:

1 cup sharp cheddar cheese, grated
Paprika

In a large bowl, mix main ingredients and pour into a greased 8-inch square baking dish.
Top with grated cheddar cheese and sprinkle with paprika.
Bake at 350°F for 35 - 40 minutes.

Serves 8.

Tomatoes Stuffed with Orzo and Feta Cheese

Serve with the Butterflied Leg of Lamb on page 53 of I've GOT to Have That Recipe!

>½ cup orzo*
>½ cup feta cheese, crumbled
>½ cup celery, chopped
>1 tsp. dillweed
>1 tsp. lemon juice
>1 tbsp. olive oil
>¼ cup green pepper, diced
>
>4 large firm tomatoes

Cook orzo according to package directions, drain well and add remaining ingredients except tomatoes.

Cut tops off tomatoes and scoop out most of the pulp. Stuff tomatoes with orzo mixture.

Set tomatoes in ¼ inch of water in a baking dish and bake at 350°F for 15 - 20 minutes. Watch carefully.

* Orzo, a rice-shaped pasta, can be found in the pasta section of your grocery store.

Serves 4.

Doreen's
Easy Baked Beans

These are NOT hotdog baked beans; these are company beans. They complement any entrée! The recipe can be doubled or tripled.

4 slices bacon
½ cup onion, chopped
1 28-oz. can Libby's Deep-Browned Beans
2 tbsp. brown sugar
1 tbsp. Worcestershire sauce
1 tsp. Dijon mustard

Cook bacon until crisp, remove from skillet (reserve drippings), drain and crumble. Set aside. Cook onions in reserved drippings until tender. Combine all ingredients, including bacon, and blend well.

Pour into a 1½-qt. casserole and bake, uncovered, at 300° - 325°F for 2 hours.

Serves 6.

Enticing
Entrées

Marinated
Pork Tenderloin

Anisette and cloves give the pork tenderloin a unique flavour. Serve with rice, orzo or buttered noodles. You'll be asked for this recipe!

⅓ cup dry sherry
⅓ cup soya sauce
⅓ cup Anisette*
⅛ tsp. cinnamon
⅛ tsp. ground cloves
1¾ lb. pork tenderloin

1 tsp. cornstarch
Water

Mix sherry, soya sauce, Anisette, cinnamon and cloves together. Pour over tenderloin and allow to marinate for 2 hours or overnight.

Place tenderloin and marinade in a shallow baking dish. Bake at 325°F for 1 - 1½ hours, basting frequently. Remove tenderloin to a warm serving platter.

Mix cornstarch with enough water to moisten it. Add to pan juices and simmer, stirring constantly, until the sauce is thickened. Pour sauce over the warm tenderloin and serve immediately.

* Anisette can be purchased in liquor stores.

Serves 4 - 6.

 # Pork Medallions
à la Tarragon and Dijon

Easy yet elegant. Serve with buttered noodles and a tossed green salad.

1¼ lb. pork tenderloin, cut into 1½-inch
  thick slices, slightly flattened
1 tbsp. Dijon mustard

2 tbsp. butter
⅛ tsp. salt, or to taste

½ cup beef broth
½ - 1 tsp. dried tarragon, crumbled
½ cup light cream
Freshly ground pepper to taste

Spread one side of meat slices with mustard.

In a heavy skillet, melt butter over medium heat and add pork medallions, mustard-side down. Sprinkle with salt. Reduce heat to low and cook for 5 minutes on each side or until no longer pink. Remove meat to a heated serving dish.

Add beef broth and tarragon to pan drippings, stirring to scrape up brown bits. Simmer for 2 minutes or until about half the liquid remains. Add cream and simmer, stirring, until sauce is slightly thickened. Season with pepper and pour over medallions.

Serves 4.

Saucy
Pork Chops

Serve this with rice as there is lots of sauce.

6 loin pork chops, $\frac{1}{2}$ inch thick

2 tbsp. flour
1 tsp. salt
$\frac{1}{2}$ tsp. pepper

Vegetable oil

1 10-oz. can condensed cream of
   mushroom soup
$\frac{3}{4}$ cup water
$\frac{1}{2}$ cup dairy sour cream
$\frac{1}{2}$ cup onion, chopped
$\frac{1}{2}$ - 1 tsp. fresh ginger root, grated
$\frac{1}{2}$ tsp. rosemary

1 3-oz. (79-g) can French-fried onions*

Trim fat from pork chops.
Combine flour, salt and pepper and coat chops in flour mixture.
In a large skillet, heat oil and quickly brown chops. Place browned chops in a 9-inch × 13-inch baking dish.
Combine soup, water, sour cream, onion, ginger and rosemary. Pour over pork chops and bake, covered, at 350°F for 50 minutes. Uncover, add French-fried onions and bake for an additional 10 - 15 minutes.

* Can be found in the potato chip section of your grocery store.

Serves 6.

Medallions of Beef with Hunter Sauce

Sauce:

> 1 cup beef bouillon (not consommé)
> 1 tsp. shallots, thinly sliced and broken
>   into rings
> 1 cup whipping cream
>
> 2 tbsp. clarified butter*
> 1 tsp. fresh garlic, minced
> 2 tsp. shallots, thinly sliced and broken
>   into rings
> ½ cup fresh mushrooms, thickly sliced
> ¼ - ⅓ cup dairy sour cream
> 3 dashes Worcestershire sauce
> ½ cup dry red wine

Meat:

> Centre section of 1 beef tenderloin**
> 2 tbsp. clarified butter
> ⅓ cup Grand Marnier liqueur

Sauce: In a small saucepan, heat bouillon and 1 tsp. shallots over medium-high heat. Add whipping cream, a little at a time, and whisk so that mixture does not curdle. Simmer for 2 minutes. (Do not boil.)

Meanwhile, in a small skillet, lightly sauté, in 2 tbsp. clarified butter, garlic, 2 tsp. shallots and mushrooms. Add to sauce. Add sour cream and Worcestershire to sauce and continue to simmer for 20 - 30 minutes. Stir in wine and simmer again until well blended. Keep warm.

Meat: Cut beef into ¾-inch-thick medallions.

In a large skillet, over high heat, sear beef in 2 tbsp. clarified butter (approximately 1 - 1½ minutes per side for medium rare). Press meat down with back of spoon to seal in juices. Add Grand Marnier and baste beef. Remove from heat.

To serve, place medallions on individual serving plates and spoon Hunter Sauce over meat.

* To clarify butter: Heat butter until it melts. When the whey (milky sediment) has separated from the melted fat, pour off the fat (clarified butter), and discard the whey.

** Ask your butcher to cut the tenderloin so that the centre can be cut into nice round medallions. (Outside sections can be used for another dish.)

Serves 3 - 4.

Peppered
Beef Tenderloin

1 - 3 lb. beef tenderloin*
Crushed lemon pepper**
1 recipe Hunter Sauce, page 59

Roll tenderloin in a generous coating of pepper. Place on a greased broiler pan and bake at 475° - 500°F until desired doneness. (Medium rare takes approximately 30 minutes. If meat springs back to the touch, it is done.)
Slice beef to desired thickness and serve with Hunter Sauce.

* Ask your butcher to trim the fat and remove the casing from the tenderloin.

** You may substitute crushed black peppercorns or seasoned black pepper for lemon pepper.

Serves 6.

Special Marinade for
Roast Beef

Try using this marinade on a Baron of Beef or Prime Rib.

2 large onions, coarsely chopped
1 clove garlic, peeled
1 cup soya sauce
2 tsp. mixed Italian herbs (marjoram,
    oregano and basil)
¼ cup gravy colouring

Combine onions, garlic, soya sauce and herbs in a blender. Process until very smooth. Stir in colouring. Store in a covered jar.
The day before serving, place roast in a plastic bag, add marinade and seal bag. Turn meat over several times and place bag in a shallow dish. Refrigerate overnight. Continue to baste during the day.
Take meat out of the refrigerator at least 1½ hours before roasting. (Meat should be at room temperature.) Roast meat in marinade until medium rare.

Yvonne's Stuffed Whole Beef Tenderloin

A dinner party must!

Stuffing:

> 3 large onions, thinly sliced
> 6 tbsp. olive oil
> 4 tbsp. butter
> 2 cloves garlic, minced
> 1 small can (4 oz./125 g) sliced ripe olives, drained
> ½ cup ham, chopped
> ½ - 1 tsp. pepper
> 1 tsp. thyme
>
> 2 egg yolks, beaten
> 2 tbsp. fresh parsley, snipped
> Salt if necessary

Roast:

> 1 large whole beef tenderloin
> Vegetable oil

Stuffing: In a large skillet, sauté onions in oil and butter until tender. Add garlic, olives, ham, pepper and thyme. Cook and stir for 2 - 3 minutes.

Stir in egg yolks and parsley. Cook and stir a few minutes more. Adjust seasonings. Set aside.

Roast: Slice tenderloin lengthwise to make 2 pieces. Place one piece of tenderloin on board and spoon stuffing on top. Cover with second piece of meat. Wrap string around roast in several places to secure.

Place roast on a rack in a baking dish. Brush with oil and bake at 300°F for 50 minutes.

Let stand for 10 minutes before slicing.

Serves 8.

Sally's
Party Pasta

This inexpensive yet delicious way to serve a crowd. Can be made in the morning and refrigerated until ready to cook. Try it instead of lasagna!

3 tbsp. vegetable oil
2½ lb. lean ground beef
2 large onions, chopped
3 cloves garlic, minced

2 28-oz. cans meatless spaghetti sauce
1 large green pepper, finely chopped
2 - 4 tbsp. brown sugar
1 tsp. oregano
1 tsp. basil

1 12-oz. pkg. broad egg noodles

2 cups dairy sour cream
3 cups Parmesan cheese, grated

2 - 3 cups mozzarella cheese, grated

In a large pot or Dutch oven, heat oil and add ground beef, onions and garlic. Cook until meat is no longer pink. Drain well.

Add spaghetti sauce, green pepper, sugar, oregano and basil to meat mixture and bring to a boil. Reduce heat, cover and simmer for at least 15 minutes.

Cook noodles according to package directions and add to spaghetti sauce mixture.

Cover bottom of two 9-inch × 13-inch baking dishes with ½-inch of sauce mixture. Spread 1 cup of sour cream over each and then sprinkle each dish with 1 cup Parmesan cheese.

Divide and spread remaining sauce between the two dishes. Sprinkle each casserole with remaining Parmesan cheese.

Top dishes with mozzarella cheese. Bake, uncovered, at 350°F for 25 minutes.

Serves 14 - 18.

Enchilada Casserole

These are as much fun as fingerpainting, so roll up your sleeves, pour yourself a glass of Sangria, and get your hands dirty. You'll love the results! Serve with Mexican Corn Bread, page 91.

2 lb. lean ground beef
1 medium onion, chopped
1 4-oz. can diced green chilies

2 16-oz. (500-mL) jars enchilada sauce
1 8-oz. jar medium salsa or taco sauce*
1 15-oz. pkg. (10) flour or corn tortillas
½ lb. sharp cheddar cheese, grated
combined with
½ lb. Monterey Jack cheese, grated

1 10-oz. can condensed cream of
mushroom soup

In a medium skillet, brown ground beef with onion. Drain. Add chilies, stir and set aside.

To Assemble: In a large bowl, mix enchilada sauce with salsa or taco sauce. Dip tortilla in sauce and place on a piece of waxed paper. Put a large spoonful of meat mixture in centre of tortilla and top with a handful of cheese. Roll tortilla up and place in a large (9-inch × 13-inch) greased baking dish. Repeat for as many tortillas as will fit into dish.

Combine mushroom soup with remaining sauce and pour over tortillas. Top with any leftover meat and cheese. (Extra grated cheese may be added on top if you wish.)

Bake at 350°F for 20 minutes or until bubbly.

* If you like it hot, substitute hot taco sauce.

Serves 6 - 8.

Di's Curry

This is a basic curry recipe to use with lamb, beef or chicken. Serve over fluffy rice, topped with condiments of your choice and plenty of ice cold beer.

¼ cup butter, divided
1 large onion, chopped
1 large apple, chopped
2 tbsp. fresh gingerroot, grated
2 cloves garlic, minced

2½ lb. (4 cups) lamb, beef or chicken cut
   into 1-inch cubes

½ tsp. turmeric
2 tsp. coriander
2 tsp. cumin
½ tsp. cinnamon
¾ tsp. cardamom
½ tsp. cloves
½ tsp. pepper
Cayenne pepper (optional)*
Grated rind of 1 orange
2 large tomatoes, coarsely chopped
1 5½-oz. can tomato paste
1 cup stock or 1 10-oz. can beef or chicken
   broth**
½ cup raisins (optional)

Condiments***

In a large Dutch oven, melt ⅛ cup butter and sauté onion, apple, ginger and garlic until onion is transparent. Remove ingredients with a slotted spoon to a separate bowl, add the remaining butter to the Dutch oven, add the meat or poultry cubes and brown. Return the onion and apple mixture to the Dutch oven, add rest of ingredients, mix well, cover and simmer over low heat for 2 - 3 hours. (We prefer to make the curry the day before, refrigerate and reheat.) Serve with rice (cooked with a pinch of saffron if you have it) and your choice of condiments.

* If you prefer hotter curry, add cayenne pepper starting with ⅛ tsp. If you prefer it fiery, add chili paste.
** You may wish to thin the sauce by adding more stock or water before serving.
*** Condiments — optional — any or all of — chutney, chopped peanuts, chopped bananas, raisins, chopped hard-cooked egg, shredded coconut, yogurt.

Serves 4. Pasta Salad with Spicy Italian Vinaigrette (*see pages 40-41*)

Judy's
Wine Stew

Simple adult fare. Serve with buttered noodles or rice.

> 2 lb. lean round steak or 2 lb. stewing
>   beef*
>
> 1 large onion, coarsely chopped
> 1 envelope of dry onion soup mix
> 1 10-oz. can condensed cream of celery
>   soup
> 10 oz. dry red wine

Cut round steak into 2-inch squares and set aside.

In a large casserole dish, with a tight-fitting lid, combine onion, onion soup mix, celery soup and wine, and blend well. Add meat, making sure it is well covered with wine-soup mixture. Cover casserole tightly with aluminum foil (very important), place lid on top of aluminum foil and bake at 350°F for 2 hours.

Variation: Pre-cooked vegetables, such as carrots, potatoes and onions, may be added at end of cooking time.

* If using stewing beef, double cooking time.

Serves 4 - 6.

Randy's Champagne Salmon (*see page 69*)

Norma's
Baked Bean Casserole

It's nice to know this is bubbling away in the oven when you come in from an outing! Serve with Indian Fry Bread, page 92.

½ lb. bacon

1 lb. lean ground beef
1 large onion, chopped
2 14-oz. cans pork and beans
1 14-oz. can stewed tomatoes
¼ - ½ cup brown sugar
1 tsp. chili powder
Salt and pepper to taste
Dash of celery salt

Cook bacon until crisp in a large skillet. Remove and drain. Crumble bacon and set aside.

Brown ground beef and onion in skillet. Drain off any excess fat. Add remaining ingredients, including bacon. Blend well and adjust seasonings to taste.

Spoon baked bean mixture into a 2-qt. casserole and bake at 300°F for 2 hours.

Serves 8.

Ethel's
Cod with Ginger and Black Bean Sauce

This recipe comes to us from Newfoundland.

> 1 lb. cod cut into large serving pieces
> Salt and freshly ground pepper to taste
>
> 3 medium onions, chopped
> ¼ cup butter
> ½ cup fresh ginger root, grated
> ¼ cup black beans*

Place cod in a large greased baking dish. Sprinkle with salt and pepper.

In a skillet, sauté onions in butter until tender. Add ginger and black beans and mix well. Remove from heat.

Top cod with onion-ginger mixture and bake, uncovered, at 350°F for 45 minutes.

* Black beans can be purchased at a Chinese grocery store.

Serves 6.

Barb's Sole

Can be made early in the day and popped in the oven a half-hour before dinner.

2 10-oz. (284-g) pkg. frozen chopped
  spinach

2½ cups fresh mushrooms, sliced
2 - 3 tbsp. butter

1½ cups dairy sour cream
2 tbsp. lemon juice
2 tbsp. flour
1 tsp. salt
Freshly ground pepper to taste
½ tsp. tarragon, crushed
2 tbsp. dry white wine or vermouth

1½ lb. sole fillets
2 tbsp. butter
Paprika
Lemon pepper

   Thaw spinach, drain and set aside.
   In a medium skillet, sauté mushrooms in 2 - 3 tbsp. butter for
2 - 3 minutes. Set aside.
   In a bowl, combine sour cream, lemon juice, flour, salt, pepper,
tarragon and wine. Blend well. Mix one-half of the sour cream mixture
with the spinach. Spread spinach mixture in a 9-inch × 13-inch
baking dish. Top spinach with mushrooms. Arrange sole fillets on top,
overlapping as necessary. Spread on the other one-half of the sour
cream mixture. Dot with 2 tbsp. butter and sprinkle with paprika and
lemon pepper. Bake at 375°F for 25 - 30 minutes.

Serves 6.

Randy's
Champagne Salmon

Randy came to our house and made this wonderful dish for us. We wish Randy could come to your house — but here's the recipe anyway!

1 lb. salmon fillet, skin on, deboned

1 split of champagne*
1 tsp. shallots, finely sliced
1 tsp. butter

1 cup whipping cream
⅓ cup dairy sour cream
½ tsp. Worcestershire sauce

Fresh parsley for garnish

Cut salmon fillet into 4 serving pieces. Set aside.

Heat a large skillet until very hot. Add champagne and shallots and bring to a boil. Boil for 3 minutes. Add 1 tsp. butter.

Place salmon pieces, skin-side down in the champagne. Using a spoon, baste salmon until it becomes slightly less than pink, about 3 - 4 minutes. (Deliberately undercook.) Remove salmon from skillet, place on a dinner plate and invert another dinner plate on top. (This will keep the salmon warm while you make the sauce, but not cook it.)

To make sauce, whisk whipping cream gradually into champagne. Simmer over medium heat for 2 - 3 minutes. (Do not boil.) Stir in sour cream and Worcestershire sauce. Continue to cook and stir until sauce is thickened and reduced (5 - 10 minutes).

Pour any juices from salmon (sitting on plate) into sauce. Continue to reduce sauce by increasing heat slightly.

Skin salmon (skin should peel off easily) and add salmon to sauce. (Feed skin to your cat.) Baste until salmon is hot.

To serve, garnish with parsley.

* It isn't necessary to buy expensive champagne.

Serves 2 - 4.

Karen's
Salmon and Cheddar Cheese
Soufflé with Dill Sauce

Dill Sauce:

½ cup mayonnaise
⅓ cup sour cream
1 tsp. Dijon mustard
1 tsp. tarragon wine vinegar
1 tsp. dillweed
Salt and freshly ground pepper to taste

Soufflé:

3 tbsp. butter
2 tbsp. green onions, minced
3 tbsp. flour
1 cup milk or light cream
½ tsp. oregano
Salt and freshly ground pepper to taste
1 tbsp. tomato paste
4 eggs, separated
1 7½-oz. can salmon, drained and flaked
½ cup white sharp cheddar cheese, grated

Dill Sauce: Blend all ingredients together and set aside.

Soufflé: In a skillet, melt butter and sauté onions over medium heat for 1 - 2 minutes. Stir in flour and gradually add the milk or light cream, stirring constantly until mixture is smooth and thickened. Add oregano, salt and pepper to taste and tomato paste. Beat egg yolks separately and stir into mixture. Add the salmon and cheese and blend well.

In a separate bowl, beat egg whites until stiff and fold gently but thoroughly into the salmon mixture. Pour into a greased casserole dish and bake at 375°F for 30 minutes or until the soufflé is lightly browned and firm to the touch. Serve immediately with dill sauce.

Serves 4

Pat's Fillet of
Salmon in Phyllo Pastry

Salmon:

6 sheets phyllo pastry
¾ - 1 cup butter, melted
6 salmon fillets (4 oz. each)

Dillweed
Salt and freshly ground pepper
6 tsp. butter

Sauce:

4 tbsp. butter
2 cups fresh mushrooms, sliced
2 tbsp. flour
1½ - 2 cups light cream
1 tsp. dry mustard
Salt and freshly ground pepper
¼ cup sherry

Salmon: Separate one sheet of phyllo pastry, spread out and generously brush with melted butter. Place one salmon fillet along narrow edge of phyllo pastry, leaving a 2-inch border on the narrow edge. Generously season salmon with dillweed, salt and pepper and dot with 1 tsp. butter. Fold border over salmon, fold in edges and roll up pastry, generously brushing with butter as you fold. Place phyllo bundle in a buttered baking dish, being sure all sides are well brushed with butter. Repeat procedure until all fillets are wrapped. (This can be done early in the day and refrigerated until ready to bake.)

Bake at 400°F for 20 minutes or until phyllo is golden brown. Top with mushroom sauce and serve immediately.

Sauce: In a skillet, melt the butter and sauté mushrooms until tender. Stir in the flour and gradually add the cream, stirring constantly. Add mustard, salt and pepper to taste. Add sherry and stir and simmer for 1 - 2 minutes until thick and bubbly. Serve immediately over salmon bundles.

Serves 6.

 # Brian's Shrimp
with Tomatoes and Feta

Delicious — all you need is a crusty loaf of bread and a bottle of Greek wine. Serve it directly from the skillet.

4 tbsp. butter
½ medium onion, finely chopped

1½ cups canned tomatoes, drained and
   chopped in chunks
½ cup dry white wine
2 tbsp. fresh parsley, snipped
½ tsp. oregano

30 medium-sized shrimp, shelled with tail
   on and deveined

Salt and freshly ground pepper to taste

2 - 3 oz. feta cheese, cubed

    Melt butter in a heavy skillet, add onions and sauté until transparent. Add tomato chunks, wine, 1 tbsp. parsley and oregano. Increase the heat and bring to a gentle boil, stirring gently until the tomato mixture reduces, approximately 5 - 7 minutes. Add shrimp and cook over medium heat until shrimp are cooked. (Do not overcook the shrimp — 5 minutes should be long enough.) Season with salt and pepper, drop the cubed pieces of cheese into the skillet, stir gently, sprinkle with remaining parsley and serve immediately.

Serves 4 for a snack, 2 for a dinner.

Teresa's
Oriental Shrimp Casserole

Shrimp chow mein!

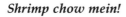

2 tbsp. butter
2 cups celery, cut diagonally
1 cup onion, chopped
1½ - 2 cups fresh mushrooms, sliced
2 cups cooked shrimp
1 8-oz. can water chestnuts, sliced and
   drained
¾ cup slivered almonds
1 6-oz. pkg. dry chow mein noodles

1 10-oz. can condensed cream of
   mushroom soup
¾ cup light cream
2 tsp. soya sauce
Paprika

Melt butter in a large skillet and lightly sauté celery, onion and mushrooms. Remove from heat and add shrimp, water chestnuts, almonds and one-half package noodles. Pour into a medium-sized (2½ qt.) greased casserole and cover with other half package noodles.
Mix soup, cream and soya sauce together and pour over noodles. Sprinkle with paprika and bake at 350°F for 40 minutes.
Variation: Diced leftover roast pork may be substituted for shrimp.

Serves 6.

Chicken
Parmigiana

Everyone loves this!

> 6 chicken breast halves, skinned, boned
>   and cut into large chunks
> 2 eggs, beaten
> 1 tsp. salt
> ½ tsp. pepper
> 1 cup bread crumbs or soda cracker
>   crumbs
> ⅓ cup vegetable oil
>
> 1 14-oz. can tomatoes
> 1 14-oz. can tomato sauce
> ½ tsp. basil
> ½ tsp. oregano
> ½ tsp. garlic powder
> 1 tbsp. butter
>
> ½ cup Parmesan cheese, grated
> ½ lb. mozzarella cheese, grated

Prepare chicken. In a small bowl, combine eggs, salt and pepper. Place crumbs in a bag. Dip chicken pieces in egg mixture and then shake in the crumbs.

Heat oil in a large skillet. Brown chicken on both sides. Remove from pan and arrange in a 9-inch × 13-inch baking dish.

In a medium saucepan, combine tomatoes, tomato sauce, basil, oregano and garlic powder. Bring to a boil and simmer for 10 minutes. Stir in butter.

Pour tomato sauce over chicken pieces. Sprinkle with Parmesan cheese. Cover and bake at 350°F for 30 minutes. Uncover and sprinkle with mozzarella. Bake an additional 10 minutes or until cheese melts.

Serves 6 - 8.

Dawn's Artichoke-and-Cheese-Stuffed Chicken Breasts

4 chicken breast halves, skinned and
   deboned

$1\frac{1}{2}$ cups mild cheddar or Monterey Jack
   cheese, grated
$\frac{1}{4}$ cup mayonnaise
2 tsp. green onions, chopped
2 tsp. dried parsley flakes
$\frac{1}{2}$ tsp. Dijon mustard
1 6-oz. jar marinated artichokes, drained

$\frac{1}{2}$ cup flour
$\frac{1}{2}$ tsp. salt
$\frac{1}{4}$ tsp. pepper

1 egg
1 tbsp. water

$\frac{1}{2}$ cup bread crumbs

$\frac{1}{4}$ cup vegetable oil

Pound chicken breasts to $\frac{1}{4}$-inch thickness.

Mix cheese, mayonnaise, onion, parsley and mustard in a small bowl. Cut artichokes into bite-size pieces and stir into cheese mixture.

In a small bowl, mix flour, salt and pepper together.

In another small bowl, mix egg and water together.

Place one-quarter of the cheese mixture on each chicken breast and roll, folding in sides as you go.

Dip chicken rolls into flour, then into egg mixture, then into bread crumbs. Cover and refrigerate for 1 hour.

Heat oven to 350°F. Place oil in a 9-inch × 13-inch baking dish and heat oil in oven for 10 minutes. Remove pan from oven and carefully roll coated chicken breasts in hot oil, using tongs.

Arrange chicken in pan, and bake for 35 minutes or until golden brown.

Serves 4.

Party
Chicken Bake

½ pkg. (1 tbsp.) dry Italian salad dressing
2 tbsp. butter, melted
8 chicken breast halves

1 10-oz. can condensed cream of
  mushroom soup
1 4-oz. pkg. cream cheese, softened
1 tbsp. fresh chives, snipped
½ cup white wine

In a large skillet, combine salad dressing with butter. Add chicken and brown slowly.

Place chicken in a greased 9-inch × 13-inch baking dish.

In a medium bowl, combine soup and cream cheese. Stir in chives and wine and blend well. Spoon sauce over chicken.

Bake at 350°F for 1 hour. Baste with sauce at least twice while cooking.

Serves 6 - 8.

Easy Curried Chicken

1 chicken cut up, or 4 chicken breast
  halves and 4 thighs
½ cup honey
½ cup Dijon mustard
1 tbsp. curry powder
2 tbsp. soya sauce
Paprika

Place chicken, skin-side down, in a greased 9-inch × 13-inch baking dish.

In a small bowl, combine honey, mustard, curry and soya sauce. Pour sauce over chicken and marinate for 6 hours in refrigerator. Turn chicken over, skin-side up, cover with foil and bake at 350°F for 1 hour.

Uncover chicken, sprinkle with paprika and bake for an additional 15 - 20 minutes.

Serves 4 - 6.

 # No Peek Chicken

An easy, everyday family dish.

> 4 tbsp. butter, melted
> 1 cup uncooked rice
> 2 tbsp. water
>
> 1 10-oz. can condensed cream of celery
>   soup
> 1 10-oz. can condensed cream of
>   mushroom soup
> $\frac{1}{2}$ cup milk
> 4 chicken breast halves and 4 thighs,
>   skinned, or 1 whole chicken, cut up
> 1 envelope dry onion soup mix

Pour melted butter into a 9-inch × 13-inch baking dish. Sprinkle rice over butter and drizzle water over rice.

In a bowl, combine cream of celery soup, cream of mushroom soup and milk. Pour mixture over rice.

Press chicken pieces into soup mixture and sprinkle with dry onion soup mix. Cover tightly with foil and bake at 325°F for $2\frac{1}{2}$ hours. No peeking!

Serves 4 - 6.

Peachy Chicken

> 6 chicken breast halves
>
> 1 8-oz. bottle Russian salad dressing
> 1 pkg. dry onion soup mix
> 1 14-oz. can sliced peaches, drain and
>   reserve juice
> 1 green pepper, chopped (optional)

Place chicken breasts in a 9-inch × 13-inch baking dish.

Combine Russian dressing, onion soup mix, peach juice and green pepper. Pour over chicken breasts. Arrange peach slices on top and bake, uncovered, at 350°F for 1 hour or until done.

Variation: Substitute 1 14-oz. can apricots for peaches.

Serves 4 - 6.

# Ida's
Buttermilk Chicken

This is an overnight recipe.

2 lb. chicken, cut up
4 cups buttermilk

½ cup butter, melted
¼ tsp. tarragon or thyme
1½ tsp. lemon juice

1½ cups fine bread crumbs
¼ cup sesame seeds
2 tbsp. fresh parsley, snipped
1½ tsp. seasoned salt

Cover chicken with buttermilk and refrigerate overnight.
When ready to prepare chicken, pour off buttermilk and set chicken on paper towels to drain.
In a shallow dish, combine melted butter with tarragon and lemon juice.
In another shallow dish, combine bread crumbs, sesame seeds, parsley and seasoned salt.
Dip chicken in melted butter mixture and roll in crumb mixture.
Place chicken in a greased baking dish and bake at 350°F for 1½ hours.

Serves 4.

Turkey and
Wild Rice Casserole

What do you do with leftover turkey?

> 1 pkg. 8-oz. (200-g) long-grain and wild
>   rice
>
> 2 tbsp. butter
> 1 small onion, chopped
> 1 - 1½ cups fresh mushrooms, sliced
> 3 cups cooked turkey, diced
> ½ cup chicken broth (can make with
>   bouillon cube)
> 1 cup whipping cream
> 1 10-oz. can water chestnuts, sliced and
>   drained
> Salt and pepper to taste
>
> 1½ cups sharp cheddar cheese, grated

Prepare rice according to package directions and set aside.

In a large skillet, melt butter and sauté onion and mushrooms. Add turkey, chicken broth, cream, water chestnuts, salt, pepper and cooked rice. Blend well.

Spoon mixture into a greased 9-inch × 13-inch baking dish. Cover and bake at 350°F for 30 minutes. Uncover, sprinkle with cheese and bake, uncovered, for an additional 20 minutes.

Serves 6 - 8.

 # White Chili

Start the night before.

 1 lb. (500 g) white beans

 6 chicken bouillon cubes
 6 cups water
 2 cloves garlic, minced
 1 onion, chopped

 1 onion, chopped
 1 tbsp. vegetable oil
 2 4-oz. cans diced green chilies
 2 tsp. ground cumin
 1½ tsp. oregano
 ¼ tsp. ground cloves
 ¼ tsp. cayenne pepper
 7 cups chicken, cooked and cut into
    chunks

 3 cups Monterey Jack cheese, grated
 Parsley to garnish

Soak beans overnight in water and in the morning drain well.

In a large soup pot, early in the day, combine beans, bouillon cubes, water, garlic and onion. Bring to a boil, then reduce heat and simmer until beans are very soft, about 3 hours or more. Add more water if necessary.

In a skillet, sauté second onion in oil until tender. Add chilies and seasonings and mix thoroughly. Add to bean mixture. Add chicken and simmer for 1 hour.

Serve in bowls topped with grated cheese and garnished with parsley.

Serves 8 - 10.

Rice, Eggs
and Cheese

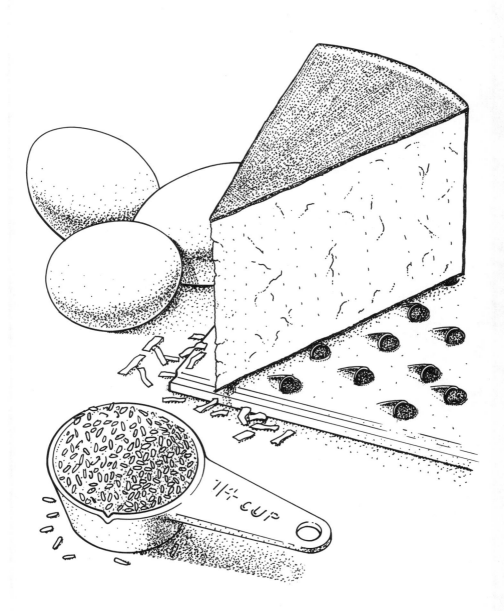

Risotto

This is an easy dish that requires gentle stirring. It is best when made with tender, loving care, so pour yourself a glass of wine, turn up the music and stir and stir and stir — you'll be glad you did!

> ¼ cup butter
> 1 large onion, finely chopped
> 1½ cups orzo* or long-grain white rice
> ½ cup dry white wine
> 2 10-oz. cans chicken broth
> ¼ tsp. saffron** (optional)
> 2 - 3 oz. Asiago*** or Parmesan cheese,
>   freshly grated
> Salt and pepper to taste
> Butter

In a large skillet, melt butter, add onion and cook and stir until tender. Add orzo or rice and stir to coat. Add wine, 1 can of chicken broth and saffron. While stirring, bring to a boil, reduce heat and stir and simmer until most of the liquid has been evaporated. Add rest of chicken broth, stir and simmer for approximately 20 minutes, or until liquid has been absorbed, but orzo or rice is not dry.

Stir in Asiago or Parmesan, salt and pepper to taste and a little extra butter if required. Serve immediately.

* Orzo can be purchased in the pasta section of your grocery store.
** If you have saffron in your cupboard — great — use it, but don't go out and buy it just for this recipe. It is very expensive.
*** Asiago is similar to Parmesan cheese and we prefer it for this recipe.

Serves 4 - 6.

Golden
Spinach Squares

1 cup onion, chopped
2 10-oz. (284-g) pkg. frozen chopped
  spinach
1 8-oz. (250-g) pkg. Velveeta cheese, cubed
2 cups cooked rice
4 eggs, beaten
⅛ tsp. pepper

In a saucepan, combine onion and spinach and cook according to package directions. Drain well. Combine with remaining ingredients.

Pour into a greased 9-inch square baking dish and bake at 350°F for 25 minutes. Cut into squares to serve.

Serves 8 - 10.

Brown Rice Casserole

3 cups chicken broth
½ tsp. basil
1 tsp. dillweed
Pinch thyme
Salt and freshly ground pepper to taste
1 cup brown rice (uncooked)

2 - 3 tbsp. butter
1 small onion, sliced
1 clove garlic, minced
½ green pepper, chopped
5 - 6 mushrooms, sliced
1 large tomato, cut into large cubes

½ cup Monterey Jack or Mozzarella
  cheese, grated

In a saucepan, combine broth, basil, dillweed, thyme, salt, pepper and rice. Cover and cook for 50 - 60 minutes or until stock is absorbed.

In a skillet, melt butter and sauté onion, garlic and green pepper for 5 minutes, add mushrooms and continue cooking until slightly tender. Blend onion mixture with cooked rice, add tomato cubes and place in a buttered casserole. Bake at 375°F for 25 minutes covered, remove lid, add cheese and cook for an additional 5 minutes or until cheese is melted.

Serves 6.

Artichoke and Chicken Crêpes

Make ahead for your next luncheon and serve with a crisp green salad dressed with Honey Garlic Dressing, page 30, I've GOT to Have That Recipe!

Crêpe Batter:

⅔ cup flour
2 eggs
3 tbsp. melted butter, slightly cooled
⅛ tsp. salt
1 cup milk

Chicken Filling:

5 tbsp. butter
½ cup onion, chopped
1½ cups fresh mushrooms, sliced
3 tbsp. flour
⅔ cup chicken broth
½ cup light cream
1 14-oz. can artichoke hearts, drained
2 cups cooked chicken, diced
⅓ cup Parmesan cheese, freshly grated
¼ tsp. rosemary
½ tsp. salt

Sauce:

¼ cup flour
⅔ cup sherry
1 10-oz. can chicken broth
2 cups light cream
½ tsp. salt
Dash of pepper

Topping:

½ cup Swiss cheese, grated

Crêpe Batter: In a medium bowl or in a blender, combine flour, eggs, butter, salt and ½ cup milk. Beat until smooth and add remaining milk. Beat well, cover and refrigerate for at least 3 hours. Make crêpes and set aside.

Filling: In a large skillet, over medium heat, melt 2 tbsp. butter. Add onions and mushrooms and cook until tender. Stir in remaining butter. Sprinkle in flour and stir until bubbly. Gradually add chicken broth and cream and cook until mixture thickens and boils, stirring constantly. Remove from heat.

Cut artichokes into bite-size pieces. Add artichokes, chicken, Parmesan cheese, rosemary and salt to mixture. Combine well. Cool.

Sauce: In a small saucepan, blend flour with sherry. Stir in broth, cream, salt and pepper. Over medium heat, bring to a boil, stirring constantly. Reduce heat, simmer and stir for 2 minutes.

To Assemble: Place ¼ cup of filling on each crêpe and roll up. Arrange seam-side down in a buttered baking dish. Pour sauce over crêpes and sprinkle with Swiss cheese. Bake at 425°F for 15 minutes.

Serves 6 - 8.

Spanish Rice

We really had to dig deep into Grandma's recipe box to find this tasty, old-fashioned recipe! It can be made ahead and reheated.

½ lb. bacon, diced
¼ cup bacon drippings
⅔ cup uncooked white rice
3 tbsp. green pepper, chopped
3 tbsp. onion, chopped
1 tsp. salt
Pepper to taste
1 28-oz. can whole tomatoes, undrained

In a large skillet, brown bacon until nearly crisp. Pour off fat except for ¼ cup.

Add rice, green pepper, onion and seasonings to skillet. Sauté until rice is light brown. Add tomatoes with their liquid, breaking them up with a fork into small chunks. Cover and simmer for 45 minutes.

Serves 6.

Three Cheese Strata

Great for brunch or lunch, along with a salad and rolls!

1 lb. farmer's cheese, grated
8 oz. feta cheese, crumbled
2 cups small curd cottage cheese

4 eggs
1 tsp. sugar

1 lb. phyllo pastry*
1 cup butter, melted

In a large bowl, mix cheeses together until well blended.

Combine eggs and sugar in a separate bowl and beat well with an electric beater. Fold egg mixture into cheese mixture and stir until smooth and creamy.

In a greased 9-inch × 13-inch baking dish, place 2 folded sheets of phyllo pastry. Brush pastry with some of melted butter. Cover with one-quarter of the cheese mixture. Repeat, layering the phyllo and cheese mixture, ending with the phyllo and melted butter.

Bake, uncovered, at 350°F for 30 — 40 minutes or until golden brown and crispy. Let stand for 10 minutes before cutting.

* Freeze remainder of phyllo.

Serves 6 - 8.

From the Bakery

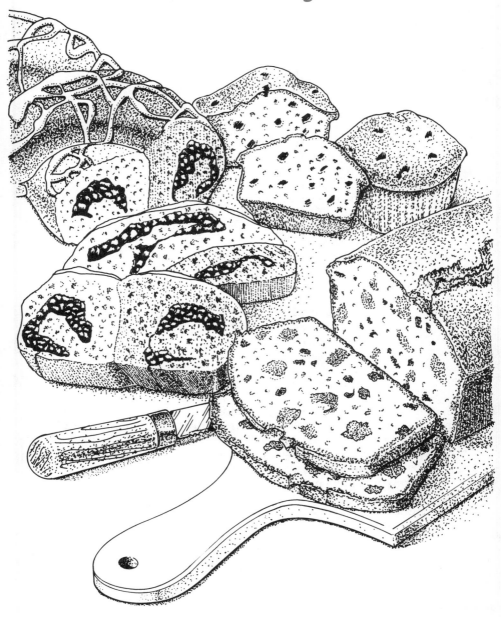

Italian Flat Bread

We have generally avoided putting yeast breads in the book, because they are a little tricky, but this flat bread is so-ooooo good we decided to test you!

Bread:

> 1 cup mashed potatoes
> 1 cup warm water
> 1 tbsp. honey
> 1 pkg. dry yeast
>
> 3 - 4 cups flour
> 2 tsp. salt
> 3 tbsp. olive oil

Spice Topping:

> ¼ cup olive oil
> 1 - 2 cloves garlic, crushed
> ½ cup Parmesan cheese, grated
> 2 tsp. oregano
> 1 tsp. basil
> ⅓ cup green onion, chopped

Bread: In a large bowl, combine potatoes and warm water. Stir in honey and yeast. Let stand at room temperature for 15 minutes. Add 1 cup flour, stirring vigorously, then blend in salt and oil. Gradually beat in remainder of flour. (Just enough flour to make a soft dough.)

On a lightly floured board, place dough and knead until smooth and elastic, approximately 5 minutes. Add flour if necessary. Place the dough in a greased bowl, cover with a cloth and let rise in a warm place until double in bulk, approximately 1 hour. Punch dough down and if necessary work in more flour (dough should not be sticky). Allow dough to rest for 10 minutes.

On a lightly floured board, roll dough into a rectangle (approximately 12 inches × 15 inches). Place on a greased baking sheet and make deep indentations in the dough every inch. (Your thumb works well for this.)

Spice Topping: In a small bowl, combine oil and garlic and brush over dough. In another small bowl, combine Parmesan, oregano, basil and green onion, and sprinkle over dough. Let dough rise in a warm place for approximately 30 minutes.

Bake at 450°F for 15 minutes or until lightly brown and crispy around the edges. Serve warm, cut into squares or strips.

Makes one 12-inch × 15-inch flat bread.

Herb and Cheese Bread

1 loaf white frozen bread dough, thawed

2 tbsp. fresh parsley, snipped
2 tbsp. onion flakes, toasted
$\frac{1}{4}$ tsp. garlic powder
$\frac{1}{4}$ tsp. freshly ground pepper
1 tsp. Italian herb seasoning
3 tbsp. Parmesan cheese, grated

2 tbsp. butter, melted

Thaw bread dough according to package instructions.

In a small bowl, combine parsley, onion flakes, garlic powder, pepper, herb seasoning and Parmesan cheese and set aside.

On a lightly floured board, roll bread dough into a rectangular shape. Brush on melted butter and sprinkle on herb-cheese mixture. Roll up dough, jellyroll fashion. Pinch edges to seal and place in a greased loaf pan, pinched side down. Cover and let rise in a warm place until double in bulk, about 2 hours.

Bake at 375°F for 35 minutes or until golden brown. Serve warm.

Makes 1 loaf.

Onion
Sage Bread

A crusty pizza-type flat bread, made in a food processor.

1 pkg. dry yeast
½ cup warm water

2½ cups flour
½ tsp. salt
½ cup cold water

1 medium onion, peeled and quartered
1 tsp. sage
3 tbsp. olive oil

Dissolve yeast in warm water in a 2-cup measure. Set aside.

Combine flour and salt in a food processor bowl. Add cold water to yeast mixture. With motor running, pour in yeast mixture and continue to process until dough comes away from sides of bowl. Process for 1 minute more to knead dough. Place the dough in a greased bowl, cover with a cloth and let rise in a warm place for 1½ hours.

Process onion with metal blade until finely chopped. (Drain if necessary.) Add sage to onion and mix well.

Oil a 12-inch × 15-inch baking sheet with 1 tbsp. olive oil.

On a floured board, punch down dough and knead in onion-sage mixture. Let rest for 10 minutes, covered. Press dough into baking sheet and brush with remaining 2 tbsp. oil. Let rise for 15 minutes.

Bake at 400°F for 25 - 30 minutes or until crisp. Cut into squares.

Serves 8 - 10.

Helen's Irish Soda Bread

Serve hot, right out of the oven!

4 cups flour
1½ tsp. salt
2 tbsp. sugar
2 tsp. baking powder
1 tsp. baking soda

1 tbsp. cold butter
2 cups buttermilk
1 cup currants (optional)

In a large bowl, mix together dry ingredients. Cut in butter. Add buttermilk and mix gently until moistened. Add currants if you wish.

Place dough on a lightly floured board and knead gently. Form into a ball and place dough on a lightly floured baking sheet. Score top with a cross and bake at 375°F for 40 - 50 minutes.

Makes 1 loaf.

Mexican Corn Bread

This spicy bread is delicious with Enchilada Casserole, page 63.

1 cup flour
1 cup cornmeal
1 tbsp. baking powder
½ tsp. salt
⅛ tsp. cayenne pepper*
1½ tsp. cumin

1 egg
2 tbsp. butter, melted
⅔ cup dairy sour cream
⅔ cup milk

⅓ cup green onions, chopped
⅔ cup canned corn kernels, drained
1¾ cups sharp cheddar cheese, grated
(reserve a handful for the top)

In a large bowl, combine flour, cornmeal, baking powder, salt, cayenne pepper and cumin.

In another bowl, beat egg, add butter, sour cream and milk and blend well.

Add dry ingredients to egg mixture, blend well and then add green onions, corn and cheese and mix together. Pour or spoon batter into a greased loaf pan, top with reserved grated cheddar cheese and bake at 350°F for 40 - 50 minutes or until done.

* If you prefer it hot, add more cayenne pepper.

Makes 1 loaf.

# Indian Fry Bread

This version of Indian Fry Bread comes to us from an Indian band in north-central Oregon. It's a delicious deep-fried bread used as an historic staple in the area. Enjoy it as they do to complement any meal — particularly on the days you are not counting calories!

3 cups flour
2 tbsp. baking powder
1 tbsp. sugar
1 tsp. salt
2 tbsp. lard
1 cup plus 1 tbsp. water

Vegetable oil for frying

Mix together dry ingredients. Add lard and rub mixture with fingers until coarse crumbs form. Add 1 cup water and stir with fork until dough clings together. If it is too dry add 1 tbsp. more water. Place dough on a lightly floured board and knead 1 - 2 minutes or until dough is smooth. If dough is still sticky, add a little more flour. Divide dough into eight equal portions, shape each portion into a ball or pat on a floured board into a pancake shape (6-inch round).

Heat 1 - 1½ inches of oil to 375°F. Place a round of dough in hot oil and cook until golden brown on one side (approximately 1 - 1½ minutes), turn and cook other side until golden brown. Remove from oil and drain on a piece of paper towel. Continue frying until all pieces are done.

Serve immediately or reheat in a single layer on a baking sheet in a 375°F oven for 5 minutes.

Serving suggestion: We like this bread hot, right out of the pan, but we also use the fry bread to make taco shells, topped with meat, refried beans, cheese, tomatoes, olives, avocados, sour cream and chives. It also complements any hearty dish, such as Norma's Baked Bean Casserole, page 66, or White Chili, page 80.

Makes 8 large fry breads.

Margaret's Cinnamon Loaf

This is a wonderful recipe. Thanks, Margaret!

⅓ cup margarine
1 cup sugar
2 eggs, well beaten
1 tsp. vanilla
1 cup sour milk*

2 cups flour
½ tsp. salt
½ tsp. soda
1 tsp. baking powder

½ cup brown sugar, packed
2 tsp. cinnamon

In a large bowl, cream margarine and sugar. Add eggs, vanilla and milk and blend well.

In another bowl, combine flour, salt, soda and baking powder and gradually add to egg mixture.

In a small bowl, combine brown sugar and cinnamon.

Spoon one-third of the batter into a greased loaf pan and sprinkle with one-third of the sugar-cinnamon mixture. Repeat twice, ending with sugar-cinnamon.

Bake at 350°F for 45 minutes, or until done.

* To make sour milk, add 1 tbsp. lemon juice or 1 tbsp. vinegar to 1 cup milk.

Makes 1 loaf.

Becca's
Sticky Cinnamon Buns

Start the night before. They're best hot, right out of the oven.

Dough:

>2 loaves white frozen bread dough

Filling:

>$\frac{1}{2}$ cup sugar
>4 tsp. cinnamon
>$\frac{1}{4}$ cup butter, softened
>$\frac{1}{3}$ cup pecans, chopped
>$\frac{1}{3}$ cup raisins (optional)

Syrup:

>$\frac{1}{2}$ cup light brown sugar
>$\frac{1}{2}$ cup corn syrup
>4 tbsp. butter
>2 tsp. cinnamon
>
>36 pecan halves

Dough: Remove dough from package, cover with waxed paper or damp tea towel and thaw the night before baking.

Filling: In a small bowl, combine sugar and cinnamon.

Turn thawed dough out onto lightly floured board. Roll dough into a 16 x 12-inch rectangle. Spread with butter, sprinkle with sugar-cinnamon mixture, pecans and raisins if desired.

Starting from long edge, roll up, jellyroll fashion. Pinch edges to seal. Cut crosswise into $1\frac{1}{2}$-inch slices. Place slices on a greased baking sheet. Cover and let rise in a warm place until double in bulk, about 2 hours.

Bake at 350°F for 20 - 25 minutes or until golden brown.

Syrup: While buns are baking, combine all syrup ingredients in a small saucepan. Bring to a boil, over medium heat, stirring constantly. Remove from heat and brush or spread syrup over baked buns.

Garnish each bun with 3 pecan halves. Let stand for 5 minutes before removing buns to a wire rack.

Makes 9 - 12 buns.

Cherry Pecan Bread

¾ cup sugar
½ cup butter
2 eggs

2 cups flour
1 tsp. baking soda
½ tsp. salt

1 cup buttermilk
1 cup pecans, chopped
1 10-oz. jar maraschino cherries, drained
    and chopped
1 tsp. vanilla

Glaze:

1 cup icing sugar
1 - 2 tbsp. milk or reserved cherry juice

In a large bowl, cream together sugar, butter and eggs until light and fluffy.

Combine dry ingredients and add to butter mixture along with the buttermilk. Beat until well blended. Stir in pecans, cherries and vanilla.

Pour batter into a greased loaf pan. Bake at 350°F for 55 - 60 minutes. Remove from pan, cool and glaze.

Glaze: Combine icing sugar and milk or reserved cherry juice until smooth. Drizzle over warm pecan bread.

Makes 1 loaf.

 # Strawberry Bread

1 cup butter
1½ cups sugar
4 eggs

3 cups flour
¾ tsp. cream of tartar
½ tsp. baking soda

1 cup strawberry jam
½ cup dairy sour cream
1 tsp. vanilla
1 tsp. lemon juice
1 tsp. grated orange peel

½ cup chopped nuts (optional)

In a large bowl, cream butter and sugar. Beat in eggs, one at a time, until mixture is light and fluffy.

Combine dry ingredients and set aside.

Combine remaining ingredients except nuts and add alternately with dry ingredients to butter mixture. Stir in nuts if desired. Pour into 2 greased loaf pans.

Bake at 350°F for 60 minutes or until done. Cool before removing from pan.

Makes 2 loaves.

Indian Fry Bread (*see page* 92)

Pineapple Zucchini Bread

3 eggs
2 cups sugar
1 cup vegetable oil
3 cups zucchini, grated and drained
1 8-oz. can crushed pineapple, drained
2 tsp. vanilla or almond extract

3 cups flour
½ tsp. salt
1 tsp. baking powder
2 tsp. baking soda
1½ tsp. cinnamon
1 tsp. nutmeg
1 cup nuts, chopped
1 cup raisins

In a large bowl, beat eggs, add sugar and oil and beat until light and fluffy. Add zucchini, pineapple and extract and mix well.

In another bowl, combine flour, salt, baking powder, baking soda, cinnamon and nutmeg and blend well. Add to egg mixture. Stir nuts and raisins into batter.

Pour into a greased bundt pan.

Bake at 350°F for 60 - 70 minutes or until done.

Variation: One 8-oz. can applesauce may be substituted for pineapple.

Makes 1 bundt pan loaf.

Cranberry Muffins (*see page 101*)

Apple Streusel Muffins

Muffins:

1½ cups flour
1 cup sugar
2 tsp. baking powder
2 tsp. cinnamon
1 tsp. baking soda
¼ - ½ tsp. nutmeg
2 medium apples, peeled and diced
½ cup pecans, chopped

2 eggs
½ cup buttermilk
½ cup margarine, melted

Topping:

½ cup flour
⅓ cup brown sugar, packed
1 tsp. cinnamon
¼ cup butter, melted

Muffins: In a large bowl, mix flour, sugar, baking powder, cinnamon, soda and nutmeg. Add apples and pecans and toss to coat.

In a small bowl, beat eggs, buttermilk and melted margarine until blended. Add to flour mixture and blend until just moistened. Spoon into paper-lined muffin tins and top with streusel topping.

Topping: In a small bowl, mix flour, brown sugar and cinnamon together. Add melted butter and mix until crumbly.

Bake muffins at 400°F for 20 minutes.

Makes 12 muffins.

 # Banana Chocolate Chip Muffins

2½ cups flour
1 tsp. baking powder
½ tsp. baking soda
½ tsp. salt

1 cup margarine, softened
1 cup sugar
1 egg, beaten
1 tbsp. instant coffee granules, dissolved
   in 1 tbsp. hot water
3 ripe bananas, mashed
1 cup chocolate chips

In a large bowl, combine flour, baking powder, baking soda and salt. Mix well and set aside.

In another bowl, cream margarine and sugar together until fluffy. Add egg, coffee liquid and mashed bananas. Combine with dry ingredients until moistened. Fold in chocolate chips.

Spoon into greased muffin tins and bake at 400°F for 20 - 25 minutes.

Makes 12 large muffins.

Chocolate Orange Muffins

1 cup sugar
½ cup butter
2 eggs, slightly beaten
Peel from 2 oranges, grated
Juice from 2 oranges to make ½ cup
½ cup dairy sour cream

2 cups flour
1 tsp. baking powder
½ tsp. baking soda
¾ cup chocolate chips

In a medium bowl, beat sugar and butter together until fluffy. Add eggs and mix well. Add orange peel, juice and sour cream. Mix well.

In another bowl, mix flour, baking powder and baking soda. Stir in chocolate chips. Add dry ingredients to butter mixture, blending just until moistened.

Spoon into greased muffin tins and bake at 375°F for 20 - 25 minutes.

Makes 12 large muffins.

Blueberry
Muffins with Streusel or Glaze

Muffins:

1 cup sugar
½ cup margarine
2 eggs, slightly beaten
1 cup dairy sour cream
1 tsp. vanilla or almond extract

2 cups flour
1 tsp. baking powder
½ tsp. baking soda
¼ tsp. salt
2 cups frozen blueberries (do not thaw)

Streusel Topping:

¼ cup granulated sugar
3 tbsp. flour
½ tsp. cinnamon
1 tbsp. butter, melted

Glaze:

¾ cup icing sugar
½ tsp. vanilla or almond extract
3 tsp. hot water

Muffins: In a large bowl, cream together sugar and margarine. Mix in eggs, sour cream and extract.

In another bowl, combine flour, baking powder, baking soda and salt. Mix frozen blueberries into flour mixture.

Combine dry and liquid ingredients. Spoon into greased muffin tins. If you wish to use the streusel topping, it must go on before baking. Bake at 375°F for 20 - 25 minutes.

Streusel Topping: Combine all topping ingredients until mixture is crumbly. Sprinkle on top of muffins and bake.

Glaze: Mix all glaze ingredients until smooth and drizzle over baked muffins.

Makes 12 muffins.

Cranberry
Muffins

A Christmas morning treat!

> 2 cups flour
> 1 cup sugar
> 1½ tsp. baking powder
> ½ tsp. baking soda
> Peel of 1 orange, grated
> 1½ tsp. nutmeg
> 1 tsp. cinnamon
> ½ tsp. ginger
> ½ cup margarine
>
> ¾ cup orange juice
> 2 tsp. vanilla
> 2 eggs, slightly beaten
> 2 cups fresh cranberries, chopped
>   (can substitute frozen)
> 1½ cups pecans or walnuts, chopped

In a medium bowl, combine first 8 ingredients. Mix well. Cut in margarine until crumbly.

In a small bowl, mix together orange juice, vanilla and eggs and add to flour mixture. Stir until mixture is moistened and still lumpy. Fold in cranberries and chopped nuts.

Spoon into paper-lined muffin tins. Bake at 350°F for 25 minutes or until golden brown. Serve hot.

Makes 12 large muffins.

Good Morning
Bars

Just right when you're tired of muffins!

2 cups flour
1½ cups natural bran
1 cup oatmeal
2 tsp. baking powder
½ tsp. baking soda
¼ - ½ tsp. salt
2 tsp. orange or lemon rind, grated

1 cup butter, softened
2 cups brown sugar
2 eggs
¾ cup frozen orange juice concentrate, thawed
1 cup raisins
1 cup long-thread coconut
½ cup pecans, chopped
¾ cup salted peanuts, chopped
½ cup dried apricots, chopped
1 cup chocolate chips (optional)

In a large bowl, mix together flour, bran, oats, baking powder, baking soda, salt and orange or lemon rind. Set aside.

In another bowl, cream butter and sugar together. Add eggs and beat until fluffy. Add orange juice concentrate and mix well. Combine with flour mixture and blend.

Add remaining ingredients to the above and stir until well combined.

Press this into a greased 9-inch × 13-inch baking dish and bake at 350°F for approximately 40 minutes or until done.

Makes about 32 squares.

Sweets

Cookies

Peanut Butter
and Jam Cookies by Craig

¾ cup butter
¾ cup granulated sugar
¾ cup brown sugar
1 egg, beaten
¾ cup peanut butter
1 tsp. vanilla

1¾ cups flour
½ tsp. baking soda
½ tsp. baking powder
½ tsp. salt

Granulated sugar
Jam or jelly

In a large bowl, cream butter and sugars thoroughly. Add egg, peanut butter and vanilla and blend well.

Combine dry ingredients and add to butter mixture.

Shape dough into 1-inch balls. Roll each ball in granulated sugar. Place 2 - 3 inches apart on lightly greased baking sheets. Press thumb deeply into centre of each ball. Bake at 375°F for about 8 - 10 minutes until firm but not hard.

While still warm, spoon a small amount of jam or jelly into each thumbprint.

Makes 4½ - 5 dozen.

 # Dick's Cousin's Cherry Flips

Flips:

> ½ cup butter
> ¼ cup icing sugar
> 1 egg yolk
> 1 cup flour
> ⅛ tsp. salt
> 1 tsp. almond extract
> 12 - 18 maraschino cherries, reserve liquid
>   in bottle for icing

Cherry Butter Icing:

> 3 tbsp. butter
> 1 cup icing sugar
> 3 - 4 tbsp. cherry juice
> ½ tsp. vanilla
>
> 1½ - 2 cups pecans, chopped

Flips: In a large bowl, cream butter and sugar together until fluffy. Add egg yolk, flour, salt and almond extract. Mix well.

Pinch off a walnut-size piece of dough and flatten in palm of hand. Place a cherry in centre of dough and pull dough around cherry to form a ball. Repeat.

Place on a lightly greased baking sheet. Bake at 325°F for 10 - 15 minutes. Remove from oven and cool.

Roll flips in icing and then in nuts.

Icing: Beat all ingredients together until light and fluffy. The icing should be thin.

Makes 12 - 18 flips.

Lemon Crisps

Get out your cookie cutter on Valentine's Day!

½ cup butter, softened
1 cup sugar
2 egg yolks
1 tsp. lemon juice
2 tsp. water

1¼ cups flour
1 tsp. baking powder
½ tsp. salt
1 tbsp. grated lemon rind

1 egg white, unbeaten
Sugar

In a large bowl, cream butter and sugar together. Beat in egg yolks, lemon juice and water.

In another bowl, combine dry ingredients along with lemon rind. Add this to butter mixture until well blended. Chill dough.

Work dough with hands until pliable, then roll out very thin on a floured board. Cut into shapes and place on lightly greased baking sheets. Brush lightly with egg white and sprinkle with sugar. (Do not let egg white run over sides of cookies as it will cause them to stick.)

Bake at 375°F for 8 minutes or until lightly browned. Cool slightly before removing from baking sheets.

Makes 4 dozen cookies.

Pebe's Mom's Angel Cookies

1 cup butter or margarine
½ cup brown sugar
½ cup granulated sugar
1 egg
1 tsp. vanilla
2 cups flour
1 tsp. cream of tartar
1 tsp. baking soda
Pinch of salt

In a large bowl, cream butter and sugars together. Add egg and vanilla and beat until fluffy.

In another bowl, combine dry ingredients and mix into butter mixture.

Roll into balls (size of walnut) and place on greased baking sheets. Press cookies with a fork.

Bake at 300°F for 10 - 12 minutes or until golden brown.

Variation: Press a few Smarties on top of each cookie.

Makes 3 dozen cookies.

Auntie Beryl's Cherry Almond Shortbread

A refrigerator cookie.

> 1 cup butter
> 1 cup brown sugar
> 2 cups flour
> $\frac{1}{2}$ cup maraschino or glazed cherries, chopped
> $\frac{1}{2}$ cup blanched almonds, slivered or chopped

In a large bowl, cream butter and sugar together. Stir in flour until well blended. Add cherries and almonds. Shape into two logs. Wrap in waxed paper and chill in refrigerator.

When ready to bake, slice and place on ungreased baking sheets.

Bake at 325°F for 8 - 10 minutes.

Makes 3 - 4 dozen cookies, depending on size and thickness of cookie.

 # Big Boy Cookies

Small boys like them too!

> 3 3-oz. milk (semi-sweet) chocolate bars
> 1¼ cups pecan halves
>
> ½ cup butter at room temperature
> ⅓ cup smooth peanut butter
> ½ cup granulated sugar
> ½ cup light brown sugar, packed
> 1 egg
> 1 tsp. vanilla
>
> 1 cup plus 2 tbsp. flour
> ½ tsp. baking soda

Lightly grease two large baking sheets. Break chocolate bars into squares and cut each square diagonally in half. Set aside ½ cup pecan halves and coarsely chop remainder.

In a bowl, beat together butter, peanut butter and sugars until light and fluffy. Beat in egg and vanilla.

In another bowl, combine flour and soda, blend well and stir into butter mixture. Stir in chopped pecans.

Divide dough into 18 mounds and place on baking sheets. Push chocolate pieces and pecan halves into mounds.

Bake at 325°F for 10 - 12 minutes. Let cookies cool slightly before removing from baking sheets.

Makes 18 large cookies.

 # Auntie Gladys's Celebration Cookies

Cookies:

> 1 cup butter, softened (do not substitute)
> 1 heaping tbsp. granulated sugar
> 2 cups flour

Filling:

> Red currant jelly

Icing:

> 2 - 3 tbsp. butter
> ¾ cup icing sugar
> ½ tsp. vanilla or maraschino cherry juice
> Few drops hot water

Decoration:

> Maraschino cherries, chopped

Cookies: Put all cookie ingredients in a medium bowl. Using your hands, work butter into dry ingredients until well blended. Knead dough until mixture clings together.

Take one-quarter of the dough at a time and roll out between 2 floured pieces of waxed paper, to ⅛-inch thick. Cut into 1½-inch circles. Place on ungreased baking sheets and bake at 350°F for 6 - 8 minutes or until golden brown. (Watch carefully.)

Spread one cookie with a thin layer of red currant jelly and top with a second cookie, sandwich style. Continue until all cookies are used.

Ice top of cookies and decorate with a piece of maraschino cherry.

Icing: Beat all ingredients until smooth.

Makes 3 dozen cookies.

Almond Cookies

Delicate and delicious.

>1½ cups flour
>1½ cups ground almonds
>
>¾ cup corn syrup
>¾ cup butter
>1 cup brown sugar

In a bowl, combine flour and almonds and set aside.

In a saucepan, combine corn syrup, butter and sugar. Heat to boiling, stirring constantly. Remove from heat and stir in flour mixture. Drop by heaping teaspoons, 2 inches apart, onto a greased baking sheet.

Bake at 350°F for 5 - 6 minutes. Let stand for 1 minute before removing from baking sheet.

Makes 3½ dozen cookies.

Pecan Crispies

>1 cup butter
>2 tsp. vanilla
>1 cup icing sugar
>1⅓ cups flour
>1 cup pecans, coarsely chopped
>
>Icing sugar

In a medium bowl, combine butter, vanilla and icing sugar. Beat at high speed until fluffy. Beat in flour. Gently stir in pecans.

Press dough onto a greased baking sheet. (The thinner the batter is spread, the crispier the cookies.) Bake at 350°F for 15 minutes. Cut into squares while warm and sprinkle with icing sugar.

Makes 1 cookie sheet cut into squares.

Susie's
Whoopee Pies

This recipe for homemade Ding Dongs doubles and freezes well.

Whoopee Pies:

> ½ cup margarine
> 1 cup sugar
> 2 egg yolks
> 2 squares unsweetened chocolate or
> ⠀⠀½ cup cocoa
> 1 tbsp. butter
> 2 cups flour
> 1 tsp. baking soda
> 1 tsp. salt
> 1 cup milk

Filling:

> ½ cup butter or margarine
> 2 cups icing sugar
> 2 egg whites
> ¼ tsp. salt
> 1 tsp. vanilla

Whoopee Pies: In a large bowl, cream margarine and sugar together. Add egg yolks and blend well.

In a saucepan, melt chocolate and butter together and add to sugar mixture.

Combine flour, baking soda and salt and add to mixture alternately with milk. Blend well. Drop dough by heaping tablespoons, 3 inches apart, onto a greased baking sheet.

Bake at 325°F for 10 minutes or until done. Cool. Put two whoopee pies together, sandwich style, with lots of filling in centre.

Filling: Beat all filling ingredients together until fluffy.

Makes 1 dozen large whoopee pies.

Darcy's
Tin Roof Sundae Bars

Simply irresistible!

Base:

> 2 15-oz. boxes fudge brownie mix
> ½ cup very hot water
> ½ cup vegetable oil
> 1 egg

Topping:

> 1 7-oz. jar marshmallow creme
> 1½ cups salted peanuts
> 1¾ cups semi-sweet chocolate chips

In a large bowl, combine brownie mix, hot water, oil and egg. Beat 50 strokes with a spoon. Spread into a greased 9-inch × 13-inch pan. Bake at 350°F for 28 to 30 minutes. Do not overbake.

Remove from oven and immediately spread marshmallow creme over base. Sprinkle evenly with peanuts and top with chocolate chips.

Return to oven for 2 minutes or until chocolate chips are melted.

Cool completely and cut into bars.

Makes 1 9-inch x 13-inch pan.

Cherry Jewel Bars

Base:

> 1¼ cups flour
> ½ cup brown sugar
> ¾ cup butter

Topping:

> 1 egg
> ⅓ cup brown sugar
> 1½ cups salted peanuts or mixed nuts,
>   chopped
> 1½ cups maraschino cherries, well drained
>   and chopped
> 1 cup semi-sweet chocolate chips

Base: In a medium bowl, mix flour and brown sugar. Cut in butter until crumbly. Press mixture into an ungreased 7-inch × 10-inch or a 9-inch square pan. Bake at 350°F for 15 minutes.

Topping: In a medium bowl, beat egg and stir in brown sugar, nuts, cherries and chocolate chips. Spoon topping over baked base and press down firmly. Bake at 350°F for 20 minutes.

Makes 1 7-inch × 10-inch pan.

Doreen's Bars

Kids love to make these treats — everyone loves to eat them.

> 3 68-g. Mars Bars
> ⅓ cup butter
> 3 cups Rice Krispies
> 2 cups chocolate chips

In a large saucepan, cut up Mars Bars and melt with butter. Stir in Rice Krispies and press mixture into an 8-inch × 8-inch buttered pan.

Melt chocolate chips and spread on top of Rice Krispie mixture. When chocolate sets, cut into squares.

Makes 8 - 10 portions.

Lawson's
Chewy Chocolate Peanut Bars

2 cups rolled oats
1 cup graham wafer crumbs
$\frac{3}{4}$ cup brown sugar
$\frac{1}{4}$ tsp. baking soda
$\frac{1}{2}$ cup salted peanuts

$\frac{1}{2}$ cup corn syrup
$\frac{1}{2}$ cup butter, melted
1 tsp. vanilla

1 6-oz. pkg. semi-sweet chocolate chips
$\frac{1}{2}$ cup peanut butter

In a large bowl, combine oatmeal, crumbs, sugar, baking soda and peanuts. Mix well.

In another bowl, combine corn syrup, melted butter and vanilla. Stir into oatmeal mixture and mix well. Press into a lightly greased 9-inch × 13-inch pan and bake at 375°F for 15 - 20 minutes.

In a saucepan, melt chocolate chips and peanut butter together. Spread over warm bars.

Makes 1 9-inch × 13-inch pan.

Jane's
Reese's Peanut Butter Bars

Tastes like a candy bar!

1 cup butter
1 cup peanut butter
$2\frac{3}{4}$ cups icing sugar
$\frac{1}{2}$ cup graham wafer crumbs
$1\frac{3}{4}$ cups (12 oz.) semi-sweet chocolate
  chips

In a large bowl, mix together butter, peanut butter, icing sugar and graham crumbs until well blended. Press into an ungreased 9-inch × 13-inch pan.

In a saucepan, melt chocolate chips and spread on top of peanut butter mixture. Cut into squares before chocolate becomes hard. Refrigerate.

Makes 1 9-inch × 13-inch pan.

 # Buttertart Squares

Base:

> 1 cup flour
> 2 tbsp. icing sugar
> $\frac{1}{2}$ cup butter

Topping:

> $1\frac{1}{4}$ cups brown sugar
> 2 eggs, beaten
> 1 tbsp. vanilla
> $\frac{1}{2}$ tsp. nutmeg
> 1 cup raisins
> $\frac{1}{2}$ cup chopped nuts (optional)

Base: In a medium bowl, combine flour and sugar. Cut in butter until mixture is crumbly. Press into a greased 9-inch square pan. Bake at 325°F for 10 minutes.

Topping: In a medium bowl, combine all topping ingredients and mix until well blended. Pour over baked crust. Increase oven to 350°F and bake for 30 - 40 minutes.

Variation: For Currant Squares, add $\frac{1}{2}$ cup coconut instead of nuts and 1 cup currants instead of raisins.

Makes 1 9-inch square pan.

Oatmeal Caramel Squares

½ cup butter
1½ cups rolled oats
¾ cup flour
½ cup brown sugar
½ tsp. baking soda
¼ tsp. salt

1 6-oz. pkg. semi-sweet ch   chips
½ cup walnuts, chopped
½ cup caramel ice-cream t
2 tbsp. flour

In a medium saucepan, melt butter ov   rate heat. Remove from heat, add oatmeal, flour, sugar, bakii   and salt and mix well. Press three-quarters of this mixture into   d 9-inch square pan, reserving rest of mixture. Bake at 350°F fc   utes.

Remove from oven and sprinkle with c   chips and walnuts. Mix together topping with 2 tbsp. flour. L   aramel mixture over top of chocolate chips and nuts. Sprinkle   naining oat mixture. Bake at 350°F for 15 - 20 minutes or until   rown. Cool and chill.

Makes 1 9-inch square pan.

Pebe's Lemon Bars Deluxe

2 cups flour
½ cup icing sugar
1 cup butter

4 beaten eggs
2 cups sugar
⅓ cup lemon juice
¼ cup flour
½ tsp. baking powder

Icing sugar

Sift flour and icing sugar together. Cut in butter until mixture clings together. Press into a 9-inch × 13-inch pan. Bake at 350°F for 20 - 25 minutes.

In a bowl, beat together eggs, sugar and lemon juice. Combine flour and baking powder and stir into egg mixture. Pour over crust and bake at 350°F for 25 minutes. Sprinkle with icing sugar.

Makes 1 9-inch × 13-inch pan.

Eleanor's
Date Almond Bars

David Foster loves these because they are his Mom's!

Base:

> 1 cup flour
> 2 tbsp. icing sugar
> ½ cup butter
> ½ tsp. almond flavouring (optional)

Topping:

> ½ lb. dates
> 1 cup water
> 2 tbsp. brown sugar
> 1 tsp. lemon juice
>
> ¾ cup graham wafer crumbs
> 1 tsp. vanilla
> 1 egg, beaten

Icing:

> ⅓ cup butter
> 1½ cups icing sugar
> 1 tsp. almond flavouring
> Few drops of hot water
>
> ½ cup sliced almonds, toasted

Base: In a medium bowl, mix together flour and icing sugar. Cut in butter until crumbly. Add flavouring. Press into a greased 9-inch square pan and bake at 350°F for 10 minutes.

Topping: Mix together dates, water, sugar and lemon juice in a medium saucepan. Bring to a boil and then simmer for 5 minutes or until dates are softened. Remove from heat and add crumbs, vanilla and egg. Spread over cooked base and bake at 350°F for 25 minutes. Cool and ice.

Icing: In a medium bowl, cream butter and beat in remaining icing ingredients, except almonds, until fluffy. Decorate top with toasted almonds.

Makes 1 9-inch square pan.

Olive's
Matrimonial Cake

Three mothers-in-law, three great recipes. The sugar in the filling varies from 1 tbsp. to ½ cup - your choice.

Date Filling:

> 2 cups dates, chopped
> 1 tbsp. brown sugar*
> ½ tsp. cinnamon
> 1 cup boiling water
> 1 tsp. lemon juice

Crumb Mixture:

> 1 cup flour
> ½ tsp. baking soda
> ½ tsp. salt
> 1 cup brown sugar, lightly packed
> 2 cups rolled oats
> ¾ cup butter or margarine

    Date Filling: Combine all ingredients except lemon juice in a saucepan. Cook over medium heat until soft and smooth. Stir in lemon juice and set aside to cool.

    Crumb Mixture: In a large bowl, combine all ingredients, cutting in butter until it resembles coarse crumbs. Press half of crumb mixture in bottom of lightly greased 8-inch square pan. Cover with date filling and remaining crumbs.

    Bake at 350°F for 25 - 30 minutes or until golden brown. Cool before cutting into squares.

* Sugar may vary from 1 tbsp. to ½ cup in filling, depending upon your taste.

Makes 1 8-inch square pan.

Perfect
Endings

Cakes and Icings

Mrs. Farquhar's
Viennese Chocolate Cake

The flavour is well worth the effort!

Cake:

½ cup sugar
¾ cup milk
2 oz. unsweetened chocolate

½ cup butter
1 cup sugar
2 eggs, well-beaten

½ cup milk
½ tsp. vanilla

1⅓ cups flour
2 tsp. baking powder
¾ tsp. cinnamon
⅛ tsp. cloves
Pinch of salt

Icing:

2 egg whites
1 cup brown sugar
3 tbsp. cold water

⅓ cup butter
1 oz. unsweetened chocolate, melted
½ tsp. vanilla

Cake: In a small saucepan, combine ½ cup sugar, ¾ cup milk and 2 oz. chocolate. Heat until sugar and chocolate are melted. Boil gently for exactly 2 minutes, stirring constantly. Cool to lukewarm.

In a large bowl, cream butter and sugar together. Add eggs. Add chocolate mixture, one-third at a time, beating well after each addition.

Combine milk and vanilla in a measuring cup and set aside.

Mix together all dry ingredients and add alternately with milk to batter. Pour batter into 2 greased and waxed-paper-lined, 8-inch layer cake pans.

Bake at 325°F for 25 minutes or until done. Cool and ice.

Icing: In top of a double boiler, over boiling water, beat egg whites, sugar and water until frosting stands in peaks. Remove from heat, cover pot with damp cloth and cool.

In a medium bowl, cream butter, chocolate and vanilla. Fold in egg white frosting, one-third at a time.

Spread lavishly between layers and then ice rest of cake.

Makes 8 - 10 portions.

Chocolate Chip Date Cake

Cake:

> 1¼ cups boiling water
> 1 cup dates, chopped
>
> ¾ cup shortening
> 1 cup sugar
> 2 eggs
>
> 2 cups flour
> 1 tsp. baking soda
> ½ tsp. salt
> 1 tbsp. cocoa
>
> 1 cup chocolate chips

Topping:

> ¼ cup brown sugar, packed
> ½ cup chopped nuts
> 1 cup chocolate chips

Pour boiling water over dates in a small bowl. Mix together; set aside to cool.

In a large bowl, cream shortening and sugar. Add eggs and beat well.

In a small bowl, combine flour, baking soda, salt and cocoa. Add to shortening mixture alternately with date mixture, adding the dry ingredients first and last. Stir in chocolate chips. Pour into a greased 8-inch square cake pan.

Combine topping ingredients and spread over batter. Bake at 350°F for 35 minutes or until done.

Makes 8 - 10 portions.

Fudgie
Almond Torte

Sinfully rich!

Cake:

> 1 tsp. instant coffee granules
> 2 tbsp. hot water
> 4 oz. semi-sweet chocolate, melted
>
> 3 eggs, separated
>
> ½ cup butter
> ¾ cup sugar
> ¼ cup almond paste*
> ½ cup flour

Glaze:

> 4 oz. semi-sweet chocolate
> 1 tbsp. butter
>
> ½ - ¾ cup toasted slivered almonds for
>   garnish

Cake: Dissolve coffee granules in hot water. Stir in melted chocolate.
  In a medium bowl, beat egg whites until stiff but not dry and set aside.
  In another bowl, cream butter and sugar together. Beat in almond paste until well blended. Mix in egg yolks, chocolate-coffee mixture and flour. Fold in beaten egg whites, one-third at a time, until just blended. Spread into a greased, 8-inch round cake pan.
  Bake at 350°F for 30 minutes or until done. Do not overbake. Cool on rack for 10 minutes before removing from pan.
  Glaze: In top of a double boiler, over simmering water, melt chocolate and butter together. Spread on cake and garnish with toasted almonds. Refrigerate to set glaze.
  Serve at room temperature.

* Buy almond paste in your bakery.

Serves 8 - 10.

Louise's
Orange Chiffon Cake

We've included this recipe because it is a traditional childhood birthday cake that we've always enjoyed.

Cake:

> 2¼ cups flour
> 1½ cups sugar
> 3 tsp. baking powder
> 1 tsp. salt
>
> ½ cup vegetable oil
> 5 egg yolks, unbeaten
> Rind of 2 oranges, grated
> Juice of 2 oranges plus enough water to
>   make ¾ cup
>
> 6 egg whites or 1 cup egg whites
> ½ tsp. cream of tartar

Icing:

> ⅓ cup butter
> 1½ cups icing sugar
> ½ tsp. vanilla extract
> 2 - 3 tbsp. orange juice
> 1 tsp. orange rind, grated

In a large bowl, combine dry ingredients. Make a well in centre and add oil, egg yolks, orange rind and juice. Beat well.

In another bowl, beat egg whites and cream of tartar until stiff. Fold into cake mixture until just blended.

Line the bottom of a tube pan with waxed paper and pour batter into pan. Bake at 325°F for 60 minutes.

Ice with orange icing.

Icing: In a bowl, cream butter and icing sugar together. Add vanilla, orange juice and rind, and beat until smooth. Spread on cooled cake.

Makes 8 - 10 portions.

Lemon Cake

Cake:

> 1 small pkg. lemon gelatine
> 1 cup boiling water
> ¾ cup corn oil
> 4 eggs, slightly beaten
> 1 pkg. lemon cake mix

Lemon Drizzle:

> 5 tbsp. lemon juice
> 2 tbsp. butter, melted
> 1½ cups icing sugar

Cake: Dissolve gelatine in boiling water. Cool slightly.

In a large bowl, add oil, eggs and cake mix. Add gelatine mixture and beat for 3 minutes. Pour into a greased and floured tube or bundt pan. Bake at 350°F for 45 minutes.

Serve plain or with lemon drizzle

Lemon Drizzle: Mix all ingredients together until smooth and spoon over warm cake.

Makes 8-10 portions.

Apple Cake

Good warm or cold, but try it warm with whipped cream — delicious!

> 2 eggs
> 1½ cups vegetable oil
> 2 tsp. vanilla
>
> 3 cups flour
> 2 cups sugar
> 2 tsp. cinnamon
> 1 tsp. salt
> 1 tsp. baking powder
> 4 cups apples, peeled and chopped
> 1 cup pecans or walnuts, coarsely
>   chopped

In a small bowl, beat eggs, oil and vanilla. Set aside.

In a large bowl, combine flour, sugar, cinnamon, salt and baking powder. Stir in apples and pecans to coat. Add egg mixture and mix until well blended.

Spread batter evenly into an ungreased 9-inch × 13-inch pan. Bake at 375°F for 55 minutes.

Makes 1 9-inch × 13-inch pan.

Janie's
Hawaiian Wedding Cake

Aloha!

> 1 19-oz. can crushed pineapple, drained
> and juice reserved

Cake:

> 1 pkg. yellow cake mix
> Reserved pineapple juice
> 2 eggs

First Topping:

> 1 pkg. vanilla instant pudding mix
> 1 cup milk
> 8 oz. cream cheese, softened

Second Topping:

> 1 large container Cool Whip
> 1 - 1½ cups coconut, toasted

Drain and reserve juice of pineapple. Add water to juice to make 1½ cups of liquid. Reserve crushed pineapple for topping.

Cake: In a large bowl, combine cake mix, 1½ cups liquid and eggs. Beat well. Pour into a greased bundt or 9-inch × 13-inch pan. Bake at 350°F for 35 minutes or until done. Cool completely.

First Topping: In another bowl, mix pudding with milk and add cream cheese. Beat until smooth and well-blended. Stir in crushed pineapple and pour on top of cooled cake.

Second Topping: Frost cake with Cool Whip and sprinkle with coconut. Refrigerate.

Serves 12 - 16.

Auntie Ethel's Cupcakes

An old-fashioned flavour for an everyday cupcake!

2 cups flour
1 tsp. baking soda
1 tsp. salt
1 tsp. cinnamon
1 tsp. nutmeg

½ cup raisins
½ cup nuts, chopped

½ cup shortening, softened
1 cup sugar
1 egg
1 tbsp. lemon rind, grated
1 cup applesauce

In a large bowl, combine dry ingredients. Add raisins and nuts.
In another bowl, cream shortening and sugar together. Add egg and beat until fluffy. Stir in lemon rind and applesauce until well mixed. Add this mixture to dry ingredients and beat well.
Pour batter into paper-lined cupcake tins. Bake at 375°F for 20 minutes or until done.
If you are feeling energetic, ice with your favourite topping.

Makes 12 - 18 cupcakes.

Chris's Favourite Banana Pudding Cake

This is a recipe we use over and over again. Bet you will too!

1 pkg. yellow cake mix
1 pkg. instant banana or caramel pudding
   mix
½ cup ripe bananas, mashed
4 eggs
1 cup water
¼ cup vegetable oil

In a large bowl, combine all ingredients and beat for 3 minutes. Pour into a greased bundt or tube pan.

Bake at 350°F for 50 - 55 minutes.

Cool 15 minutes before removing from pan.

Variation: Drizzle with 1 cup icing sugar mixed with 1 - 2 tbsp. milk.

Makes 8 - 10 portions.

Gail's
Porridge Cake

This delicious porridge cake, served at Sea Breeze Lodge on Hornby Island, B.C., is one of their favourites — ours too!

Cake:

> ½ cup margarine, softened
> 1 cup granulated sugar
> 1 cup brown sugar, packed
> 2 eggs
> 1 tsp. vanilla
> 1½ cups flour combined with 1 tsp.
>   baking soda
> 1 - 1¼ cups porridge (leftover from
>   morning), or 1¼ cups boiling water
>   mixed with 1 cup quick-cooking oats

Topping:

> ¼ cup butter, melted
> ½ cup brown sugar, packed
> 3 tbsp. cream or evaporated milk
> ¾ cup coconut

Cake: In a large bowl, cream margarine and sugars together, then add eggs and vanilla. Beat well. Stir in remaining ingredients until well mixed. Pour into a greased 9-inch square pan. Bake at 350°F for 50 minutes.

Topping: Combine all topping ingredients and spread over warm cake. Place under broiler for 2 - 3 minutes. Watch carefully.

Makes 1 9-inch square pan.

Audrey's
Hot Water Sponge Cake

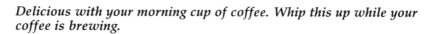

Delicious with your morning cup of coffee. Whip this up while your coffee is brewing.

Cake:

> 2 eggs, beaten
> 1 cup sugar
> 1 tsp. vanilla
> 1 cup flour
> 1 tsp. baking powder
> ½ cup boiling water with 1 tbsp. butter in
>   it

Topping:

> 1 cup brown sugar, packed
> 6 tbsp. butter, melted
> 4 tbsp. cream
> 1 cup coconut
> 1 handful of cornflakes

   Cake: In a large bowl, beat eggs, sugar and vanilla together. Combine flour with baking powder and add to batter. Beat in water and butter. Pour into a greased 8-inch square pan and bake at 375°F for 30 minutes.
   Topping: Cream all topping ingredients together and spread over warm cake. Place under broiler for 2 - 3 minutes. Watch carefully.

Makes 1 8-inch square pan.

Sheila of Sheet Harbour's Sultana Cake

Our Grannies love this cake with their tea!

> 1 lb. sultanas
> ½ cup rum
>
> 1 cup butter
> 1¼ cups sugar
> 3 eggs, beaten
> 2½ cups flour
> 1 tsp. baking powder
> 1 scant cup warm milk
> 1 tsp. vanilla
> 1 tsp. lemon peel, grated
> 1 cup citron
> 1 cup glazed or maraschino cherries,
>   chopped

The night before making the cake, steam sultanas slowly for 15 - 20 minutes and then soak in rum.

The next day, cream butter and sugar together. Add eggs and beat until light and fluffy. Combine flour and baking powder and add to egg mixture alternately with milk. Blend well. Add vanilla and lemon peel. Stir in sultanas, citron and cherries.

Pour batter into a greased and floured tube pan and bake at 350°F for 1¼ hours or until done. Cool in pan before removing.

You may add more rum by poking cake with meat fork and slowly pouring rum over the top.

Makes 18 - 20 portions.

# Poppy Seed Cake

1 pkg. yellow cake mix
1 pkg. banana instant pudding mix
½ cup vegetable oil
4 eggs
1 cup warm water

¼ cup poppy seed

1 tbsp. sugar
1 tbsp. cinnamon

Icing sugar

In a large bowl, combine the first 5 ingredients and beat for
3 minutes. Stir in poppy seeds. Pour into a well-greased bundt
or tube pan.

In a small bowl, combine sugar and cinnamon and swirl into batter.
Bake at 300°F for 60 minutes or until done. Dust with icing sugar.

Serve with whipped cream laced with Kahlua or try our Grand
Marnier Sauce, page 145, *I've GOT to Have That Recipe!*

Makes 8 - 10 portions.

Penuche Icing

*This is delicious on all cakes, but we particularly like it as an icing for
our Hot Milk Sponge Cake, page 116, I've GOT to Have That Recipe!*

½ cup butter or margarine, melted
1 cup brown sugar, packed
¼ cup milk
1 tsp. vanilla
1¾ - 2 cups icing sugar

In a medium saucepan, bring butter and brown sugar to a boil. Boil
for 2 minutes. Stir in milk and bring back to boiling point. Remove from
heat, add vanilla and cool to lukewarm. Slowly add icing sugar with an
electric beater and continue to beat until thick enough to spread.

 # Wendy's Icing

Keep this icing on hand. It lasts for six weeks in the refrigerator, freezes well and makes enough icing for three or four cakes.

> 1 lb. butter
> 1 lb. Crisco
> 1 5½-oz. can evaporated milk
> 6 cups icing sugar
> 2 - 3 tsp. vanilla

In a large bowl, beat butter, Crisco and milk together. Gradually beat in icing sugar. Add vanilla and beat until smooth.

Glaze for
Fresh Fruit Pies or Flans

When we operated Nathan's Cheesecakes, we glazed our fresh fruit toppings on cheesecakes and flans in order to keep them fresh-looking. This glaze keeps indefinitely in the refrigerator; just heat it up and use it again and again. Fruits such as strawberries, kiwis, blueberries and green grapes look and taste fresh for hours.

> 1 cup water
> ½ cup sugar
>
> 2 tbsp. unflavoured gelatine powder
> ¼ cup warm water

Bring 1 cup water and sugar to a boil in a small saucepan. Remove from heat.

Dissolve gelatine in ¼ cup warm water. Add gelatine solution to syrup. Glaze fruit with a brush.

Makes 1½ cups.

Desserts

Ginny's
Blueberry Dessert

Everybody loves this easy, make-ahead dessert!

Crust:

>2 cups graham wafer crumbs
>$\frac{1}{4}$ cup sugar
>$\frac{1}{3}$ cup butter, melted

Filling:

>2 10-oz. (300-mL) cans sweetened
>   condensed milk
>$\frac{2}{3}$ cup fresh lemon juice
>1 cup whipping cream, whipped
>4 cups fresh blueberries or frozen
>   blueberries, thawed
>
>1 cup whipping cream, whipped

   Crust: Mix together all crust ingredients and press into either a 9-inch × 13-inch pan or a 10-inch springform pan. Bake at 350°F for 5 - 10 minutes.
   Filling: Beat condensed milk with lemon juice until thick and fluffy. Fold in whipped cream and add fruit. Pour over crust and refrigerate for at least 3 - 4 hours.
   Serve topped with whipped cream.

Serves 8 - 10.

Blueberry Shortbread Crumble

Try this dessert with other seasonal fruit. It's quick and easy and you'll love the delicate flavour.

Crust:

> 2 cups flour
> 4 tbsp. icing sugar
> 1 cup butter

Filling:

> $\frac{1}{3}$ cup flour
> $\frac{1}{3}$ cup sugar
> 1 600-g. pkg. frozen, unsweetened
>   blueberries or $2\frac{1}{2}$ - 3 cups fresh
> Butter

Topping:

> $\frac{1}{2}$ cup butter, melted
> $\frac{3}{4}$ cup flour
> $\frac{1}{2}$ cup brown sugar, packed
> $\frac{1}{2}$ tsp. cinnamon
> $\frac{1}{2}$ tsp. vanilla
> $\frac{1}{2}$ cup flaked almonds

Crust: In a medium bowl, mix flour and sugar together. Cut in butter until mixture is crumbly. Press into a 10-inch pie plate or a 10-inch springform pan. Press dough up sides approximately 1 inch.
Bake at 400°F for 10 - 12 minutes.
Filling: In a large bowl, combine flour and sugar and quickly toss with blueberries. As soon as crust is out of oven, fill crust with blueberry mixture. Dot with butter and cover with topping.
Topping: In a medium bowl, combine all ingredients and sprinkle on top of blueberries.
Bake at 400°F for 30 minutes. Serve warm with ice cream or whipped cream.

Serves 8.

Ruby-Mae's
Raspberry Delight

Base and Topping:

>1½ cups graham wafer crumbs
>⅓ cup brown sugar, packed
>⅓ cup butter, melted

Filling:

>½ lb. marshmallows
>½ cup milk
>1 cup whipping cream, whipped
>2½ cups frozen raspberries, slightly
>   thawed
>⅓ cup sugar
>½ cup walnuts or pecans, chopped

Base and Topping: Mix all ingredients and put into a 9-inch × 13-inch baking dish. Bake at 325°F for 10 minutes. Reserve ¾ cup of crumbs for topping and smooth out the rest in pan.

Filling: Blend marshmallows and milk in top of double boiler. Heat over boiling water until marshmallows are melted. Cool slightly. Add whipped cream, raspberries, sugar and nuts. Pour filling over cooked base. Sprinkle reserved crumbs on top.

Refrigerate for at least 3 - 4 hours before serving.

Serves 10 - 12.

Frozen
Strawberry Dessert

Base and Topping:

> 1 cup flour
> ¼ cup brown sugar, packed
> ½ cup pecans or walnuts, chopped
> ½ cup butter, melted

Filling:

> 2 egg whites
> 1 cup sugar
> 2 tbsp. lemon juice
> 2 cups fresh strawberries, sliced
> 1 cup whipping cream, whipped

Base and Topping: In a medium bowl, combine all ingredients and then spread onto a baking sheet. Bake at 350°F for 20 minutes, stirring occasionally. Press two-thirds of crumbs into a 9-inch × 13-inch pan. Reserve remainder of crumbs for topping.

Filling: In a large bowl, combine egg whites, sugar and lemon juice. Beat until stiff peaks form. Beat in strawberries briefly. (Strawberries should be slightly broken up.) Fold in whipped cream and spoon filling over base.

Top with reserved crumbs.

Freeze for at least 6 hours before serving. Cut into squares.

Serves 10 - 12.

Rhubarb Crisp

Everybody has a favourite crisp recipe — this is ours!

Base:

> 4 cups rhubarb, chopped
> 1 cup sugar
> $\frac{1}{4}$ cup flour
> $\frac{1}{2}$ tsp. cinnamon
> $\frac{1}{4}$ tsp. nutmeg
> $\frac{1}{2}$ cup water

Topping:

> 1 cup flour
> $\frac{1}{2}$ cup rolled oats
> 1 cup brown sugar, packed
> $\frac{1}{2}$ cup butter, melted

Base: In a large bowl, mix all ingredients except water, and put into a greased 9-inch square baking dish. Pour water over base.

Topping: In a medium bowl, combine ingredients and sprinkle over base.

Bake at 375°F for 35 minutes. Serve warm with whipped cream or ice cream.

Serves 6.

Eileen's
Rhubarb Crumb Dessert

This is best with fresh rhubarb.

Base and Topping:

> 1½ cups flour
> ¾ cup butter, softened
> ¼ cup brown sugar

Filling:

> 4 cups fresh rhubarb, chopped
> 2 eggs, beaten
> 1½ cups sugar
> ½ cup flour
> ½ cup butter, melted

Sugar Topping:

> ¼ cup sugar
> ¾ tsp. cinnamon

Base and Topping: In a medium bowl, mix ingredients until crumbly. Reserve ¾ cup for topping and press remainder into a 9-inch × 13-inch pan.

Filling: Cover base with rhubarb. Combine remaining filling ingredients and pour over rhubarb.

Topping: Sprinkle reserved crumbs on rhubarb mixture.

Sugar Topping: Combine sugar and cinnamon and sprinkle on top of crumbs.

Bake at 375°F for 45 minutes or until golden brown. Serve with vanilla ice cream or whipped cream.

Serves 8 - 10.

R.C.'s
Apple Caramel
Crêpes with Rum Sauce

A dinner party favourite that can be made ahead except for the last-minute caramel.

Crêpe Batter:

> 4 eggs
> 1 cup milk
> ½ tsp. salt
> 1 tbsp. sugar
> 1 cup flour
> ½ cup butter, melted

Filling:

> 2 tbsp. butter
> ½ cup brown sugar, packed
> ½ tsp. cinnamon
> 6 - 8 medium apples, peeled, cored and
>   sliced thick
> ¼ cup pecans, chopped

Sauce:

> ¾ cup brown sugar
> 1 tbsp. cornstarch
> 1 cup water
> ½ cup butter
> ⅓ cup rum

Caramel:

> ½ cup granulated sugar

Crêpes: Batter can be made in a blender. Beat eggs until fluffy. Add milk, salt and sugar, and continue to beat while sprinkling with flour. Pour in melted butter and beat thoroughly. Cover and chill for 1 hour. Cook crêpes.

Filling: In a saucepan, melt butter and add sugar and cinnamon. Stir until melted. Add apple slices, cover and cook over low heat until apples are tender. If mixture looks too dry, add 1 - 2 tbsp. of water. Remove from heat and add pecans.

To Assemble: Fill each crêpe with ¼ cup of filling. Roll up and place in a single layer in a greased baking dish. (If making ahead, refrigerate.)

Heat the crêpes at 350°F for 15 - 20 minutes. Serve with caramel and hot rum sauce.

Sauce: In a small saucepan, combine all ingredients. Bring to a boil, stirring constantly. Reduce heat and simmer for 3 minutes. Serve hot.

Caramel: Do this at the last minute while the crêpes are heating. In a small skillet, over medium heat, cook sugar, stirring constantly until it melts and turns golden and syrupy. Immediately drizzle over heated crêpes.

Makes 16 - 18 crêpes. Serves 8.

Nana's Caramel
Bread Pudding

A comforting, old-fashioned dessert!

> 1 cup brown sugar, packed
> 4 slices buttered bread, crusts removed
>   and cubed
> 3 eggs
> 2 cups milk
> 1 tsp. vanilla
> Pinch of salt
> ¼ - ½ tsp. nutmeg

Put brown sugar in top of double boiler and add buttered bread cubes. In a small bowl, beat eggs, milk, vanilla, salt and nutmeg. Pour over bread; do not stir.

Cover and cook over gently boiling water for 1½ hours. If you don't have a double boiler, bake in a covered bowl set in a pan of water 1½ inches deep at 325°F for 1½ hours.

Serves 4.

Ted's Chocolate Coffee Bean Ice Cream Dessert

Chocolate Chip Cookies: (make ahead)

> ½ cup butter
> ½ cup brown sugar
> ¼ cup white sugar
> 1 egg
> ½ tsp. vanilla
>
> 1 cup flour
> ½ tsp. salt
> ½ tsp. baking soda
> 1 cup walnuts, coarsely chopped
> ¾ cup semi-sweet chocolate chips

Filling:

> ½ cup chocolate-covered coffee beans
> 2 pints coffee ice cream

Topping: (make the day of serving)

> 1 cup whipping cream
> 1 tbsp. sugar
> 1 tsp. coffee liqueur or very strong coffee

Chocolate Chip Cookies: In a medium bowl, cream butter and sugars well. Add egg and vanilla and beat until well blended.

Sift dry ingredients, add to butter mixture and blend well. Stir in walnuts and chocolate chips.

Drop by rounded teaspoons, 2 inches apart, onto a greased baking sheet. Flatten with a fork. Bake at 350°F for 7 minutes or until lightly browned.

Filling: Reserve 20 chocolate-covered coffee beans. Coarsely chop remainder. Soften ice cream until spreadable.

Topping: Whip all ingredients together until stiff peaks form.

To Assemble: At least 1 day ahead, grease a loaf pan and line with aluminum foil. Cover bottom with 1 layer of cookies, flat-side down, fitting together tightly.

Cover with half the ice cream, pressing down firmly. Sprinkle with chopped coffee beans. Crumble 4 cookies and sprinkle over top. Add remaining ice cream and smooth top. Top with a layer of cookies, flat-side up. Cover and freeze.

Just before serving, run knife around dessert and invert onto a plate. Ice sides and top of dessert with whipped cream mixture. Decorate with reserved chocolate coffee beans and freeze for 5 minutes.

Serves 8.

Mock Vanilla Slice

This is best prepared eight hours before serving and kept in the refrigerator. The "Sweet-Tooths" in your family will love it.

Base:

1 4½-oz. (135-g) pkg. vanilla pudding and
   pie filling mix
2 cups whipping cream
2 tsp. sugar
1 14-oz. (400-g) pkg. graham wafers

Icing:

1 cup icing sugar
2 tbsp. warmed milk
½ tsp. butter
¼ tsp. vanilla

Chocolate Drizzle:

1 1-oz. square semi-sweet chocolate
½ tsp. butter

Base: Prepare pudding according to package directions. Cool.
Whip cream and sugar together and beat until stiff.
Line an 8-inch × 12-inch baking dish with graham wafers (fitting to the edges). Pour on cooked and cooled pudding and spread whipped cream over top of pudding. Place another layer of graham wafers over top of whipped cream.
Icing: In a bowl, mix all ingredients to a liquid consistency.
Chocolate Drizzle: Melt chocolate and butter together in top of double boiler over simmering water.
Spread icing over top of graham wafers. Drizzle melted chocolate over squares and refrigerate for at least 8 hours.
Cut into squares and serve.

Serves 8 - 10.

 # Margarita Mousse

Light and delectable!

> 6 eggs, separated
> 2 cups sugar
> Grated rind of 3 limes
> ½ cup tequila
> 2 tbsp. Cointreau
>
> ½ cup lime juice (juice of 4 limes)
> 2 tbsp. unflavoured gelatine powder
> 2 cups whipping cream, whipped
>
> 1 cup whipping cream, whipped
> Shaved or curled chocolate

Using electric beater, beat egg yolks, sugar, rind, tequila and Cointreau until thick and foamy (about 5 minutes on high speed).

Pour lime juice into a small saucepan and sprinkle gelatine over top. Dissolve over low heat and then stir into mousse.

Place bowl over ice and fold in whipped cream. Stir occasionally until mixture begins to hold its shape.

Whip egg whites until very stiff and fold into mousse.

Turn into an 8- to 10-cup serving bowl. Cover and chill for at least 5 hours or overnight.

To serve, garnish with whipped cream and chocolate.

Serves 8 - 10.

Sandra's
Easy Filbert Torte

And do we mean **easy** *— made in minutes in your blender!*

Cake:

4 eggs
$\frac{3}{4}$ cup sugar
1 cup filberts or hazelnuts
2 tbsp. flour
$2\frac{1}{2}$ tsp. baking powder

Mocha Cream Filling and Icing:

$\frac{1}{2}$ cup sugar
$\frac{1}{4}$ cup cocoa
1 tbsp. instant coffee granules
$\frac{1}{4}$ tsp. salt
2 tsp. vanilla
$1\frac{1}{2}$ cups whipping cream

Garnish:

Toasted filberts or hazelnuts (optional)

Cake: Put eggs and sugar in a blender and process until smooth. Add nuts and process until finely ground. Add flour and baking powder and blend until well mixed.

Pour into two 8-inch round, greased and waxed-paper-lined layer cake pans. Bake at 350°F for 20 minutes or until done. Cool.

Filling and Icing: Place all ingredients in a blender and process until thick.

To Assemble: Divide mocha filling in half. Use one-half as filling and the other half as topping. (Don't ice sides.)

Garnish with toasted nuts if desired.

Serves 6 - 8.

Frozen
Mocha Torte

Base:

> 4 egg whites
> ½ tsp. cream of tartar
> 1 cup sugar, extra-fine or granulated

Mocha Filling:

> 4 cups whipping cream
> 3 tbsp. cocoa powder
> ½ cup sugar
> 2 tbsp. instant coffee granules

Garnish:

> Shaved or curled chocolate

Base: Cover large baking sheet with brown paper and draw three 6- to 8-inch circles on paper.

Beat egg whites and cream of tarter in a large bowl until thick and foamy. Slowly beat in sugar until thick and glossy. Do not underbeat.

Divide egg white mixture into 3 parts; shape each part into a 6- to 8-inch circle on baking sheet. Bake at 275°F for 45 minutes. Turn off oven, leave meringue in oven with door closed for 1 hour. Remove and cool.

Filling: Whip cream and add remaining ingredients. Blend carefully.

To Assemble: Fill meringue layers and frost top with mocha filling. Decorate with chocolate.

Freeze uncovered until firm, at least 3 hours. May be served immediately or wrapped in plastic wrap and returned to freezer. It keeps in freezer for up to 1 month.

Dip knife in hot water before cutting.

Serves 6 - 8.

Coffee
Velvet Ice Cream

1 egg white
2 tbsp. sugar

1¼ cups whipping cream
¼ cup sugar
1 tbsp. instant coffee granules
1 tsp. vanilla
Few drops almond extract (optional)

¼ cup almonds, finely chopped and
    toasted
¼ cup flaked coconut, toasted

In a bowl, beat egg white until foamy and then slowly add 2 tbsp. sugar. Beat until stiff peaks form.

In another bowl, whip cream and fold in sugar, coffee, vanilla and almond extract if desired.

In a small dish, combine almonds and coconut. Reserve half for garnish.

Combine meringue, whipped cream mixture and almonds and coconut.

Spoon into individual serving dishes. Sprinkle with reserved nut mixture. Freeze until firm.

Serves 4 - 6.

Chocolate-Orange Marbled Cheesecake

Rich and heavy!

Crust:

> 1 cup graham wafer crumbs
> ¼ cup sugar
> ¼ cup butter, melted
> 1 1-oz. square unsweetened chocolate,
>   melted

Filling:

> 1½ lb. (3 8-oz. pkg.) cream cheese,
>   softened
> ¾ cup light brown sugar, packed
> ¼ cup granulated sugar
> 4 eggs
> 2 cups dairy sour cream
> 2 tbsp. orange rind, grated
> 6 - 8 oz. semi-sweet chocolate, melted and
>   slightly cooled

Crust: Combine all ingredients in a small bowl. Press into bottom of a greased 10-inch springform pan. Refrigerate.

Filling: In a medium bowl, beat together cream cheese and sugars until smooth. Beat in eggs one at a time, until mixture is light and fluffy. Add sour cream and orange rind and beat until smooth. Reserve one-half of batter.

Beat cooled chocolate into remaining batter until well blended.

Spoon one-half of white batter over crust in pan. Using one-half of chocolate batter, drop four equal mounds on white batter. Repeat layers. Cut through batter with a knife in a zig-zag motion to make marble effect.

Bake at 350°F for 1 hour and 15 minutes. Check to see if cake is firm to touch. Turn off oven and leave cake in oven for 1 hour with door slightly ajar.*

Variation: Garnish with whipped cream, thinly sliced orange slices and chocolate curls.

* To ensure that oven door is only open a crack, we place a wooden spoon between the door and oven.

Serves 12 - 16.

 # Di's Piña Colada Cheesecake

Sensational flavour in a lighter than usual cheesecake!

Crust:

> 2 cups vanilla wafers, finely crushed
> 2 tbsp. sugar
> ⅓ cup butter, melted

Filling:

> 1½ lb. cream cheese, softened
> ¾ cup sugar
> 3 eggs
> ¾ cup crushed pineapple
> ¾ cup pineapple tidbits, reserve juice for
>   filling and topping
> ¼ cup reserved pineapple juice

Topping:

> 1½ cups dairy sour cream
> 2 tbsp. sugar
> 1 cup flaked coconut
> 2 tbsp. reserved pineapple juice

Garnish:

> 1 cup coconut, toasted
> Pineapple spears (optional)

Crust: In a bowl, mix all ingredients together and press into a greased 10-inch springform pan. Bake at 350°F for 5 minutes. Cool.

Filling: In a bowl, beat cream cheese and sugar together until well blended. Beat in eggs, one at a time, until mixture is light and fluffy. Stir in remaining ingredients. Pour into prepared crust and bake at 350°F for 35 - 45 minutes or until firm to touch.

Topping: While cake is baking, mix together topping ingredients. When cake is done, remove from oven and spoon on topping. Bake for an additional 5 - 10 minutes. Remove from oven and immediately sprinkle with toasted coconut. Let stand until well cooled. Refrigerate for 6 hours or overnight.

Garnish with pineapple spears if you wish.

Serves 10 - 12.

Mrs. Hirtle's
Miniature Cheesecakes

This simple but often asked for recipe freezes well.

> Butter
> Graham wafer crumbs

Cheesecakes:

> 1 lb. (2 8-oz. pkg.) cream cheese, softened
> ¾ cup sugar
> 3 egg yolks
>
> 3 egg whites

Topping:

> ¾ cup dairy sour cream
> 2½ tbsp. sugar
> 1 tsp. vanilla

Butter medium-sized muffin tins, bottoms and sides. Sprinkle with graham wafer crumbs.

Cheesecakes: In a medium bowl, beat together cream cheese and sugar until well combined. Add egg yolks and blend well.

In another bowl, beat egg whites until stiff. Fold into cheese mixture. Pour batter almost to top of muffin tins. Bake at 350°F for 15 - 18 minutes. Remove from pans and cool. (May fall slightly in centre.)

Topping: Mix together all ingredients.

Spoon topping onto cooled cheesecakes. Place on a baking sheet and bake at 400°F for 5 - 7 minutes. Cool and serve.

Makes 12 - 18.

Kath's
Almond Puff

½ cup margarine
1 cup flour
2 tbsp. water

½ cup butter
1 cup water
1 tsp. almond extract
1 cup flour
3 eggs

Glaze:

1½ cups icing sugar
2 tbsp. butter
1 tsp. almond extract
1 - 2 tbsp. warm water

Slivered almonds, toasted

Cut ½ cup margarine into 1 cup flour until crumbly. (A food processor works well.) Add water and mix until dough forms a ball.

Divide dough in half. Pat each piece of dough into a 12-inch × 3-inch strip. Set aside.

Bring ½ cup butter and 1 cup water to a rolling boil. Remove from heat and stir in almond extract and 1 cup flour. Stirring vigorously, beat in eggs, one at a time, until mixture is smooth. (Again, you can use a food processor.) Divide almond mixture in half and spread evenly over dough strips, covering completely.

Bake at 350°F for 45 - 50 minutes or until top is golden. Cool.

Glaze: Beat all ingredients together until smooth. Spread onto almond puffs and sprinkle with toasted almonds.

Serves 8.

Pies and Tarts

Mrs. P.'s
Apple Pie Crumble

What could be better on a cold winter day?

½ cup butter
⅓ - ½ cup brown sugar, packed
1 cup flour
2 tsp. cinnamon
3 tbsp. water
½ - ¾ cup pecans, chopped

6 cups apples, peeled, cored and chopped
⅓ - ½ cup granulated sugar

Whipped cream

In a medium bowl, beat butter and brown sugar until fluffy. Stir in flour, 1 tsp. cinnamon and water and blend until smooth. Add pecans and blend well.

Spread chopped apples into a greased 9-inch pie plate.

Mix granulated sugar with remaining 1 tsp. cinnamon and sprinkle over apples. Spoon pecan topping over apples in dollops.

Bake at 375°F on lowest rack in oven for 45 - 50 minutes.

Serve warm with whipped cream.

Serves 8.

Apple and Blackberry Pie

Now we know why the English love this pie!

> 1 recipe Nathan's Pastry for 2 crust pie,
> page 137, *I've GOT to Have That Recipe!*
>
> 3 lb. Granny Smith apples, peeled, cored
> and chunked (6 large apples)
> ½ cup butter
> ½ cup sugar
> Juice of ½ lemon
>
> 2 cups blackberries
> ¼ cup flour
>
> 1 egg beaten
> Sugar

Line a 10-inch pie plate with pastry.

In a large saucepan, combine apples, butter, sugar and lemon juice. Cover and allow to cook gently for about 5 minutes. Cool slightly, add berries and stir gently to combine.

Fill pie shell with apple-blackberry mixture and cover with pastry. Crimp edges, cut slits in top pastry to allow steam to escape and bake at 450°F for 10 minutes.* Reduce oven temperature to 350°F and bake for 25 minutes longer or until golden brown. Immediately brush with beaten egg and sprinkle with sugar.

* If edges of pie begin to burn, cover edges with thin strips of aluminum foil.

Serves 8 - 10.

 # Banana Split Pie

There isn't any ice cream in this Banana Split, but the kids still love it!

Crust:

> 1⅓ cups graham crumbs
> ¼ cup butter, melted
> ¼ cup granulated sugar

Filling:

> ¼ cup butter, softened
> 1 egg
> ½ tsp. vanilla
> 1 cup icing sugar
>
> 1 - 2 bananas, sliced
> 1 14-oz. can crushed pineapple, well
>   drained
> 1 15-oz. pkg. frozen sliced strawberries,
>   thawed and well drained, or fresh if
>   available
>
> 1½ cups whipping cream
> 1 tbsp. sugar
> Toasted nuts

Crust: Mix all ingredients together and press into a greased 9-inch springform pan or a 10-inch pie plate.

Bake at 325°F for 10 minutes. Cool.

Filling: In a medium bowl, beat butter, egg, vanilla and icing sugar together. Spread over cooked base. Add bananas, pineapple and strawberries in layers.

Whip the cream and sugar together. Spread over fruit and garnish with toasted nuts.

Refrigerate for 2 - 4 hours before serving.

Serves 8.

Nona's
Lemon Pie

Light, Lemony and Luscious!

> 1½ cups sugar
> ⅓ cup plus 1 tbsp. cornstarch
> 1½ cups water
>
> 3 egg yolks
> 3 tbsp. butter
> 2 tsp. lemon peel, grated
> ½ cup lemon juice
>
> 3 egg whites
> 1 9-inch baked pie shell

In a medium saucepan, mix together sugar and cornstarch. Gradually stir in water and cook over medium heat, stirring constantly. Boil for 1 minute. (This can be done in a double boiler.)

In a small bowl, beat egg yolks and add half of hot sugar mixture. Beat well and return to saucepan. Boil for 1 minute. Remove from heat and stir in butter, lemon peel and juice.

In a large bowl, beat egg whites until stiff and fold into lemon mixture. Pour filling into pie shell and refrigerate. Enjoy!

Serves 6 - 8.

 # Cherry Torte

Don't let the saltine crackers put you off this delicious dessert!

Meringue:

> 3 egg whites
> 1 tsp. vanilla
> 1 cup sugar
> ¾ cup walnuts, finely chopped
> ½ cup saltine cracker crumbs (15 crackers)
> 1 tsp. baking powder

Filling:

> 1 cup cherry juice, reserved from canned
>   cherries
> ¼ cup sugar
> ¼ tsp. almond extract
> 2 tbsp. cornstarch
> 2 14-oz. cans pitted cherries, drained
>
> 1 cup whipping cream, whipped

Meringue: Beat egg whites and vanilla until foamy. Gradually add sugar, beating until stiff peaks form. Combine remaining ingredients and fold into egg whites. Spread into a greased 9-inch pie plate, building up sides to make a rim. Bake at 300°F for 40 minutes. Cool.

Filling: Combine cherry juice, sugar, extract and cornstarch in a saucepan. Over medium heat, bring to a boil, stirring constantly. Boil for 1 minute longer or until cornstarch taste is gone. Remove from heat and add cherries. Cool.

To Assemble: Line meringue shell with half of the whipped cream. Fill with cooled cherry mixture and top with remaining cream.

Serves 8.

Sour Cream Raisin Pie

1 recipe Nathan's Pastry for 2 crust pie,
  page 137, *I've GOT to Have That Recipe!*

1 cup sugar
Dash of salt
$1\frac{1}{2}$ tsp. cinnamon
$\frac{1}{4}$ tsp. nutmeg
$\frac{1}{4}$ tsp. cloves
2 tbsp. cornstarch
3 egg yolks
$1\frac{1}{2}$ cups dairy sour cream
$1\frac{1}{2}$ cups dark seedless raisins

Milk
Sugar

Line a 9-inch pie plate with pastry.

In a medium saucepan, mix sugar, salt, cinnamon, nutmeg, cloves and cornstarch. Beat in egg yolks, then sour cream and raisins. Cook and stir over low heat for 10 minutes. Remove from heat and cool for 15 minutes. Spread filling into pie shell and top with second crust. Seal and crimp edges.

Bake at 400°F for 30 - 40 minutes or until lightly browned. For crispier crust, brush with milk and sprinkle with sugar part way through baking.

Serves 8.

Helen's
Prune Plum Tarte

What do you do with your neighbours' prune plums?

> 20 prune plums
> 1 10-inch unbaked pie shell
>
> 3 eggs
> 5 tbsp. flour
> ½ tsp. cinnamon
> ½ cup ground almonds
> ¾ cup brown sugar
> ⅔ cup cream
> 1 tsp. vanilla
>
> Whipped cream

Cut plums in half, remove pits and place cut side up in unbaked pie shell.

In a bowl, beat eggs until they are thoroughly blended. Add remaining ingredients except whipped cream and beat until smooth. Pour egg mixture into pie shell lined with plums and bake at 375°F for 30 - 40 minutes or until a knife inserted in the filling comes out clean.

Top with whipped cream.

Serves 6 - 8.

Fudge Pie

So easy, yet so good!

> 1 recipe Nathan's Pastry, page 137, *I've
>   GOT to Have That Recipe!*
>
> 3 squares unsweetened chocolate
> ½ cup butter
>
> 4 eggs
> 2 cups sugar
> 2 tsp. vanilla
> 1 5⅓-oz. can evaporated milk
>
> Whipped cream or vanilla ice cream

Line a 9-inch pie plate with pastry.

In a saucepan, melt chocolate and butter together over medium heat.

In a bowl, beat eggs. Add sugar, vanilla and evaporated milk. Mix well. Add chocolate-butter mixture and blend.

Pour filling into pie shell and bake at 350°F for 35 minutes or until firm to touch. Garnish with whipped cream or vanilla ice cream.

Serves 6 - 8.

Mrs. Dorazio's
Maid of Honour Tarts

We've been asked to dig up a recipe for good old-fashioned Maid of Honour Tarts — here it is! The recipe can be easily doubled.

1 recipe Nathan's Pastry, page 137, *I've
GOT to Have That Recipe!**

3 tbsp. butter
½ cup sugar
1 egg, separated
½ tsp. almond extract
3 tbsp. rice flour
½ cup coconut

Strawberry or raspberry jam

Roll out enough pastry to line 9 muffin-size tart shells.
In a bowl, cream together butter and sugar until light and fluffy. Add egg yolk, almond extract and rice flour. Blend well.
In another bowl, beat egg white until stiff and fold into butter mixture. Fold in coconut.
In each tart shell place 1 tsp. of your favourite jam. Top with 1 tbsp. of coconut mixture.
Bake at 375°F for 20 - 25 minutes or until golden brown.

* Freeze the remainder of the pastry or make up some Lemon Curd, page 158, to fill extra tart shells.

Makes 9 muffin-size tarts.

Auntie Beryl's Lemon Curd

We like to keep a jar of this delicious lemon curd in our refrigerator. It keeps indefinitely and has a myriad of uses. It is good spread on your morning toast or as a cake filling. When making a pie, there always seems to be leftover pastry. Simply make up a few tart shells and fill with lemon curd.

> 6 eggs
> 2 cups sugar
> 1 cup butter
> Juice of 3 lemons (½ cup)
> Rind of 3 lemons

In top of a double boiler, beat eggs until light and fluffy. Add remaining ingredients and cook until mixture is thick and smooth, stirring frequently.

Pour into glass jars and store in refrigerator.

Makes 2 - 3 cups.

Bits
and Pieces

RASPBERRY

David Else's Moose Milk

A celebration drink!

> 6 cups vodka
> 3 cups chocolate mint liqueur
> 12 cups 2% milk (we know you'll want to watch those calories!)
> Splash of soda water on top of each glass (optional)

Mix all ingredients together. Refrigerate. Serve chilled.

Makes 21 cups.

We've included in this book two quick and easy party starters that you can whip up in the blender as fast as you can say "cha, cha, cha!"

Marie's Margaritas

> 1 355-mL can frozen limeade
> 2 or more cans ice
> ½ can tequila
> ⅓ can Triple Sec

Process all ingredients until ice is well crushed. Enjoy!

Bullfrogs

> 1 can frozen limeade
> 2 or more cans ice
> 1 can vodka or white rum
> 1 can soda water

Process all ingredients until ice is well crushed. Serve in long stemmed glasses with a slice of fresh lime if you wish.

Nona's Lemon Pie (*see page 153*)

Do's Christmas
Hot Buttered Rum Mix

This makes a nice Christmas or hostess gift. Enclose a recipe card with each jar, tied with a cinnamon stick.

> 1 lb. butter
> ½ tsp. nutmeg
> ½ tsp. cinnamon
> ½ tsp. lemon rind
> 5 lb. brown sugar
> 1 cup dark rum

Allow butter to soften at room temperature until very soft.

Cream butter and add nutmeg, cinnamon and lemon rind. Add brown sugar, a cup at a time, add a little rum to slightly moisten the mixture. Continue the same way until all ingredients have been added. Transfer to clean sealing jars. Seal and keep in a cool place. DO NOT REFRIGERATE. Will keep for 4 months.

Hot Rum Toddy

Put 2 heaping tsp. of hot buttered rum mix in a mug and add 1 jigger of dark rum. Fill with boiling water and serve with a cinnamon stick!

Makes 1 cup.

 # Dr. B.'s Eggnog

We make this up Christmas Eve to serve to friends and relatives on Christmas day!

10 egg whites	13 oz. rye
½ cup sugar	18 oz. rum
	2 cups milk
10 egg yolks	
	Grated rind of 1 lemon
4 cups light cream	Grated rind of 1 orange
2 tbsp. sugar	Freshly ground nutmeg

In a large bowl, beat egg whites and sugar together until stiff.

In another bowl, beat egg yolks until very light. Combine the egg white mixture with the egg yolks and stir until blended.

In a large serving bowl, whip cream and sugar together until quite thick and fluffy. Slowly pour the egg mixture into the cream mixture, beating constantly. Add rye, rum and milk and continue to mix. Top with grated lemon and orange rind and freshly ground nutmeg. Chill several hours or overnight.

Serves 10 - 12.

Nova Scotia Eggnog

This eggnog should be made one to two weeks before serving and kept in the refrigerator.

12 egg whites	4 cups whipping cream, whipped
½ cup sugar	4 cups milk
	4 cups scotch
12 egg yolks	1 cup rum
¼ tsp. salt	
1 cup sugar	Nutmeg

In a very large bowl, beat egg whites and ½ cup sugar until stiff.

In another bowl, beat egg yolks, salt and 1 cup sugar until very light. Add egg yolk mixture to egg whites and stir until blended.

Add whipped cream, milk, scotch and rum. Mix well.

Store in refrigerator in containers. Stir before serving. Garnish with nutmeg.

Makes 20 cups.

Mickey's Almond Roca

It's taken us 27 years to get this secret recipe — so mum's the word!

1 4-oz. (125-g) milk chocolate bar, grated
1 cup blanched almonds, chopped
¾ cup pecans, finely chopped
1 cup butter, do not substitute
1 cup granulated sugar

Prepare chocolate and nuts and set aside.

Melt butter slowly in a heavy skillet (cast iron is best), over medium heat. Stir in sugar gradually, add almonds and increase heat to medium-high. STIR CONSTANTLY for 6 - 8 minutes until mixture becomes a caramel colour and nuts are lightly toasted.

Pour mixture onto an ungreased baking sheet (10 inches × 14 inches) and spread slightly. Immediately sprinkle with grated chocolate and top with chopped pecans. Pat down nuts with the back of a metal tablespoon. Cool. Break into bite-size pieces and store in sealed containers. Refrigerate.

Michelle's Homemade Poppycock

You'll have to make lots of this; it seems to keep disappearing!

6 cups popped popcorn
1 cup peanuts, salted and skinless

½ cup butter
½ cup liquid honey

In a large bowl, combine popcorn and peanuts.

In a small saucepan, melt butter, stir in honey and boil gently. Stir and cook for 2 minutes. Pour hot butter mixture over popcorn and mix well.

Spread popcorn mixture onto lightly greased baking sheet(s).

Bake at 300°F for 10 minutes, stirring occasionally. Reduce heat to 250°F and bake for 10 minutes longer.

Cool and store in airtight containers.

Makes 6 - 8 cups.

Auntie Mabel's
Mother's Mustard Pickles

This recipe is over 100 years old and so tasty!

> 6 lb. small cucumbers, cut into chunks
> 3 lb. small white onions (silverskins), peeled
> 6 large green peppers, cut into chunks
> 3 red peppers, cut into chunks
> 3 large cauliflowers, broken into flowerettes
> 1 large head celery, cut into chunks
> 1 cup coarse pickling salt
> 16 cups water

Sauce:

> 2 tbsp. turmeric
> 11 tbsp. dry mustard
> 1 tsp. cinnamon
> $\frac{1}{2}$ tsp. allspice
> $\frac{1}{2}$ tsp. ground cloves
> 2 cups flour
> $4\frac{1}{2}$ cups light brown sugar
> 2 tsp. celery salt
> 2 tsp. onion salt
> 2 cups cold water
> 16 cups cider vinegar, warmed

Mix all vegetables together. Dissolve salt in water and pour over vegetables. Let stand overnight.

Sauce: In a large canning pot, mix dry ingredients with cold water until smooth. Stir in warmed vinegar. Wash brine from vegetables, drain well and add vegetables to sauce. Cook and stir over medium heat until almost to the boil. Pour pickles into sterilized jars and seal with wax.

Makes 30 or more 8-oz. jars.

Sister Beatrice's Chutney

Sister Beatrice, who belongs to the congregation of the Sisters of St. Ann, founded in 1848, has kindly consented to share her delicious chutney recipe with us.

15 medium-sized apples (Gravenstein are
   best), peeled, cored and chopped
1 lb. raisins (3 cups)
3 large onions, peeled and chopped
3 lb. sugar (7 cups)
4 cups malt vinegar
2 oz. mustard seed (¼ cup)
16 cloves garlic, minced
½ cup fresh ginger root, grated
1 tsp. - 1 tbsp. salt to taste

Place all ingredients in a large canning pot. Over medium heat, gradually bring to a boil. Reduce heat and simmer for 3 - 4 hours, stirring occasionally. Chutney should be dark in colour and thick in consistency. Remove from heat and pour into sterilized jars. Seal and store in a cool place.

Makes 12 - 14 8-oz. jars.

John's Mustard Sauce

A recipe from the Farmhouse Inn on Galiano Island, B.C. Delicious served hot over ham.

½ cup granulated sugar
1 tbsp. dry mustard
1 egg, beaten
½ cup white vinegar
2 tbsp. butter

In a small saucepan, combine sugar, mustard and egg. Slowly stir in vinegar and cook over medium to low heat. Add butter and stir until thick.

Makes approximately 1 cup.

Ian's Marinade
for Barbecued Poultry

This recipe is enough marinade for a 3 - 4 lb. chicken cut up or 4 whole chicken breasts. We like to precook the chicken, marinate for 24 hours and barbecue 5 - 6 minutes either side, brushing with marinade.

1 tbsp. sugar
1 tsp. dry mustard
1 tsp. ginger
½ cup apple juice
⅓ cup soya sauce
¼ cup lemon juice
3 cloves garlic, minced
½ cup salad oil

Mix all ingredients together. Marinate poultry for 24 hours.

Ma Tye's
Orange Glaze for Ham

¼ cup brown sugar
2 tbsp. cornstarch
1½ cups orange juice
⅓ cup horseradish
2 tbsp. vinegar
1 tbsp. orange rind, grated

In a saucepan, mix together sugar and cornstarch, add rest of ingredients and cook over medium heat, stirring constantly until thickened and no taste of cornstarch remains. Use as a glaze for ham the last half hour of cooking.

Mrs. Sherman's Mustard Ring

This is a nice complement to ham.

> 4 eggs
> 1 cup water
> ½ cup cider vinegar
> ¾ cup sugar
>
> 1½ tbsp. gelatine
> 2 tbsp. dry mustard
> ½ tsp. turmeric
> ½ tsp. salt
>
> ⅓ cup green onions, finely chopped
> 1½ cups dairy sour cream

In a bowl, beat eggs, water, vinegar and sugar until light and fluffy.

In top of a double boiler, combine gelatine, mustard, turmeric and salt. Add egg mixture and cook and stir until slightly thick.

Cool mixture until it starts to set and then stir in onions and sour cream. Pour into a greased 4-cup mold. Refrigerate for 2 - 3 hours or until ready to serve.

Serves 8 - 10.

 # Sharon's Granola

Delicious as a snack or as breakfast cereal with milk.

> 5 cups grains — a combination of oat, rye,
>   wheat or barley flakes (we use all 4)
> 1 cup coconut
> 1 cup nuts, coarsely chopped
> 1 cup wheat germ
> 1 cup sunflower seeds
> 1 cup sesame seeds
> 1 cup raisins, dates or dried apricots
>   (optional)
>
> 1 cup liquid honey
> 1 cup safflower oil
> 1 - 2 tsp. vanilla
> 1 cup skim milk powder

In a large bowl, combine grains, coconut, nuts, wheat germ, sunflower seeds, sesame seeds and raisins. Set aside.

In a saucepan, heat honey and oil together until mixed, add vanilla and skim milk powder, and stir until smooth and blended.

Pour honey mixture over grain-seed mixture and blend well until coated.

Spread mixture on baking sheets (approximately 4). Do not crowd granola.

Bake at 250°F for 30 - 45 minutes, stirring and turning 3 or 4 times so as not to burn. If using raisins, watch that they don't burn. Granola is done when it is golden brown. Do not overcook.

Store in tightly covered container.

Makes approximately 12 cups.

 # Grandma Lillie's
Raspberry Jam

There is no Certo in this very old recipe.

Raspberries, any amount
Sugar

Put berries in a large in Dutch oven. Bring berries to a rolling boil, stirring occasionally. Boil for 3 minutes. Remove from heat and measure the amount of boiled berries. Put boiled berries back in Dutch oven and add equal cups of sugar to the amount of berries. (For example, for 6 cups boiled berries, add 6 cups sugar.)

Bring berries and sugar to another rolling boil and boil for 3 minutes. Remove from heat and beat with an electric beater for 3 minutes. (We do this outside, using newspaper under pot to catch the splatters.) Can be beaten by hand as well.

Pour hot jam into sterilized jars. Cool and top with melted paraffin. Store in a cool place.

This recipe is good for all berries.

* Rolling boil — this means berries are boiling rapidly causing a great rolling action.

Mom's Strawberry Jam

This jam tastes like fresh strawberries as long as you freeze the jam until ready to use. No Certo is necessary!

8 cups (2 qt.) strawberries, hulled
8 cups (2 qt.) boiling water

6 cups sugar

Pour boiling water over prepared strawberries and let stand for 2 minutes. Drain thoroughly.

Put strawberries and 4 cups of sugar into a Dutch oven or large pot. Bring to a rolling boil* for 2 minutes, stirring constantly. Add remaining 2 cups of sugar and again bring to a rolling boil for 5 minutes more. Stir constantly.

Pour jam 1/4-inch thick onto edged baking sheets. Cool on counter overnight. Spoon into sterilized jars or containers and freeze.

* Rolling boil — this means berries are boiling rapidly causing a great rolling action.

Makes 4 - 6 6-oz. jars.

INDEX

171

173

175